First published January, 2006 by
WORLD CLASS COACHING 15004 Buena Vista Drive, Leawood, KS 66224 (913) 402-0030

ISBN 0-9746723-9-4

Author - David Platt
Edited by Mike Saif

Front Cover - Designed by Babcock Illustration & Design.

Published by
WORLD CLASS COACHING

HOW TO PLAY AGAINST AND BEAT THE 3-5-2

This book sets out to illustrate how to effectively counter the 3-5-2 system, recognising the strengths of it and negating them as well as taking advantage of the weaknesses that it has. After a brief summary of the main components of the 3-5-2, highlighting the strengths and weakness of it, we will look at some effective tactical planning to play against and beat it and also look at ways of practicing those tactics on the training pitch, through sessions and drills designed specifically to prepare in a manner to overcome the system.

It is important to realise that each formation has its strengths and weaknesses and that at the start of each match there is 11 players against 11 players. These players, arranged on the pitch, make up the formation and each formation will cause problems for any other formation unless the players themselves perform.

In order to simplify things, I have split the pitch up into thirds, dealing with both the defensive attributes and offensive attributes in a progressive way. For ease of reference, the 3-5-2 system is always portrayed as the **Black Team with White Numbers.**

In my experience, simple instructions to players where they can carry them out on the field instinctively pay far more dividends than looking at elaborate ways to play. Simplifying each issue is fundamental if the tactical aspects are to be successful. With this in mind I like to have a symmetrical plan both when defending and attacking, with the same defensive plans and attacking schemes respectively used for whichever side of the pitch the ball is on. In this book therefore, when looking at the diagrams for coaching purposes, simply mirror the tactic shown for when the ball is on the opposite side of the pitch to the diagram.

CHAPTER 1

THE 3-5-2 SYSTEM

THE 3-5-2 SYSTEM

The 3-5-2 system evolved largely due to the fact that coaches wanted to get an extra player into the midfield area from the traditional 4-4-2 system and in order to do this they believed that a line of 3 defenders could take care of the 2 strikers that invariable played against them, giving them the opportunity to advance a player into the midfield and thus increase their chances of dominating this area. In the early stages of the 3-5-2 a sweeper was employed behind 2 marking players, but deep lying sweepers have faded away since the offside rules have been changed. As a result, the 3 defenders of the 3-5-2 now play a more zonal game, shuffling across together and marking areas rather than players, with the wing backs being responsible for defending the channels.

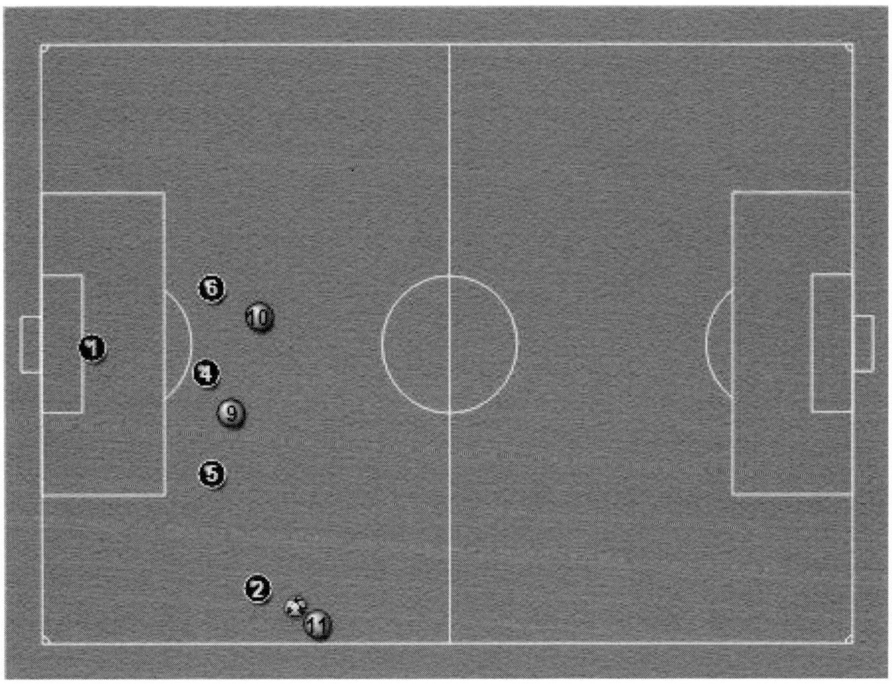

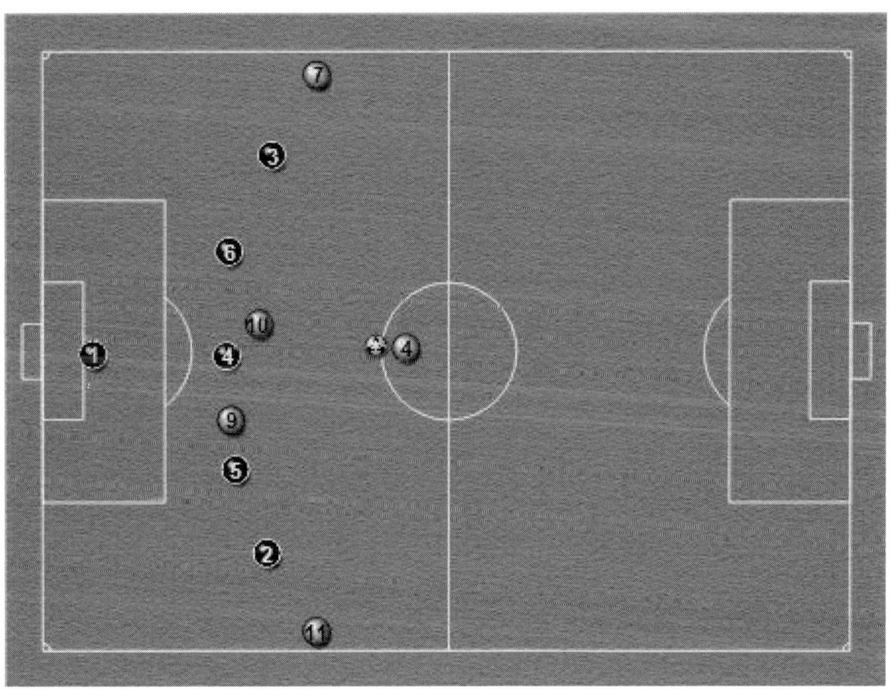

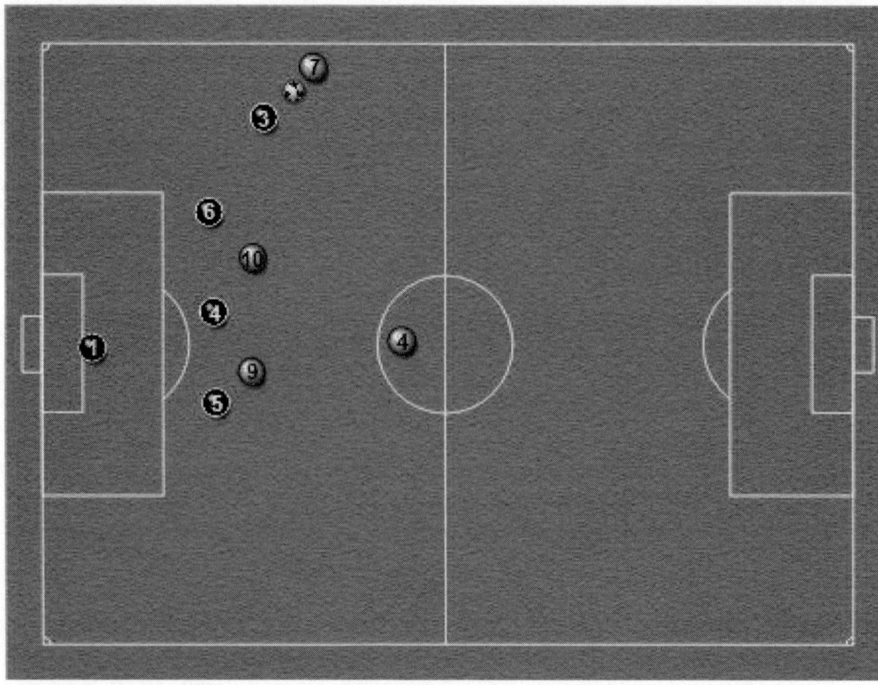

In front of these 5 players are 3 central midfielders, with one of these acting as a screen in front of the back 3, playing deeper than the other 2. Due to the fact that the wing backs are required to defend the channels, it is the job of the outside central midfielders to close the ball down when it is wide and higher up the pitch.

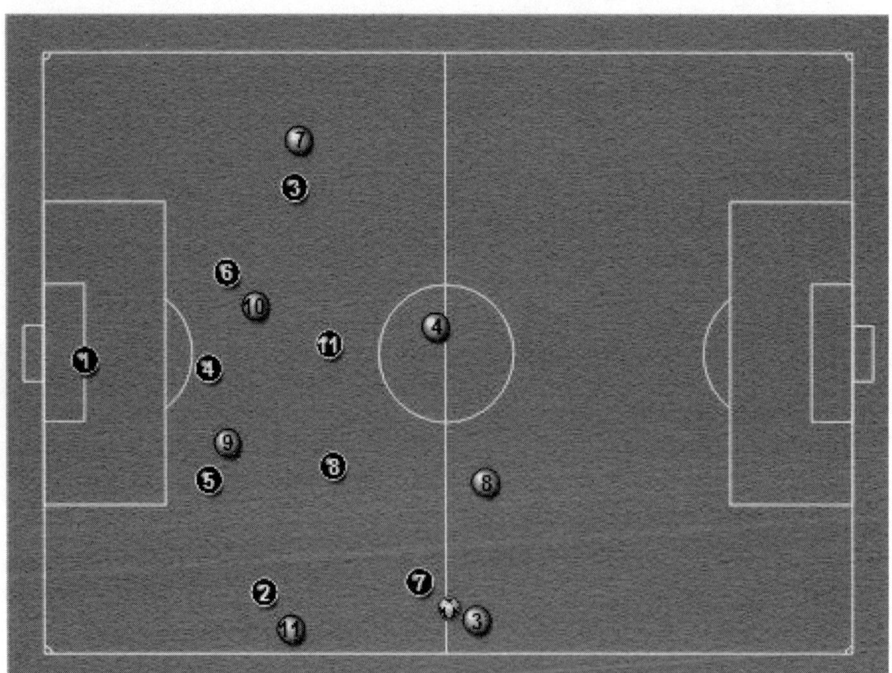

When the ball is transferred central, the anchor player has to come out to meet it with the other 2 central midfielders dropping back to cover. In effect this is inverting the initial triangle and many teams that operate with the 352 system will prefer to drop and defend deeper should this scenario happen rather than having the anchor player advance to close down as a hole appears between the back players and midfield unit that can be exploited.

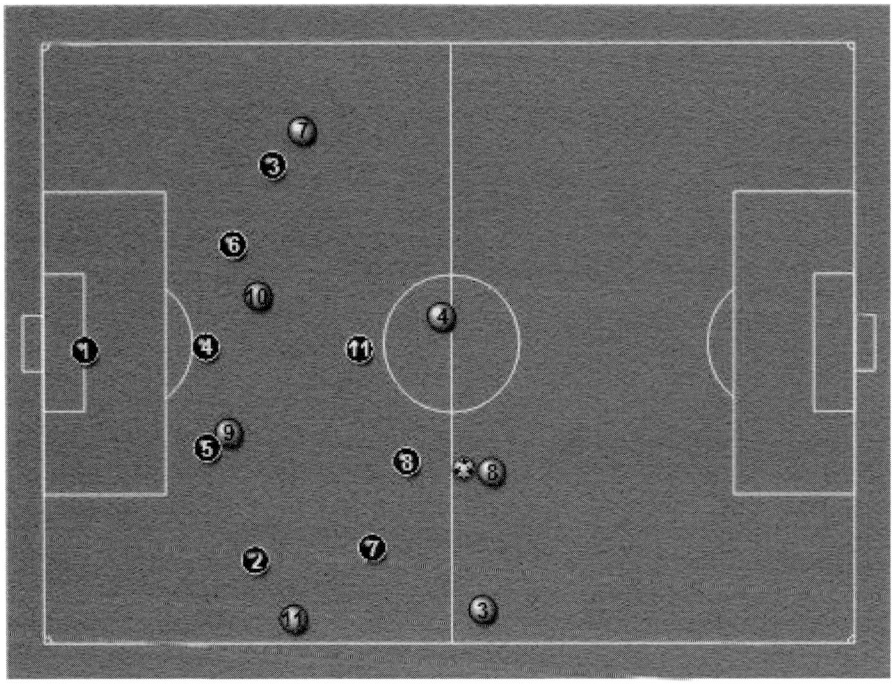

As the ball is then transferred across to the other side, the left central midfielder (11) goes to close down. If the transfer is made quickly and effectively, it is a very hard task to ask of him as he has so much ground to make up.

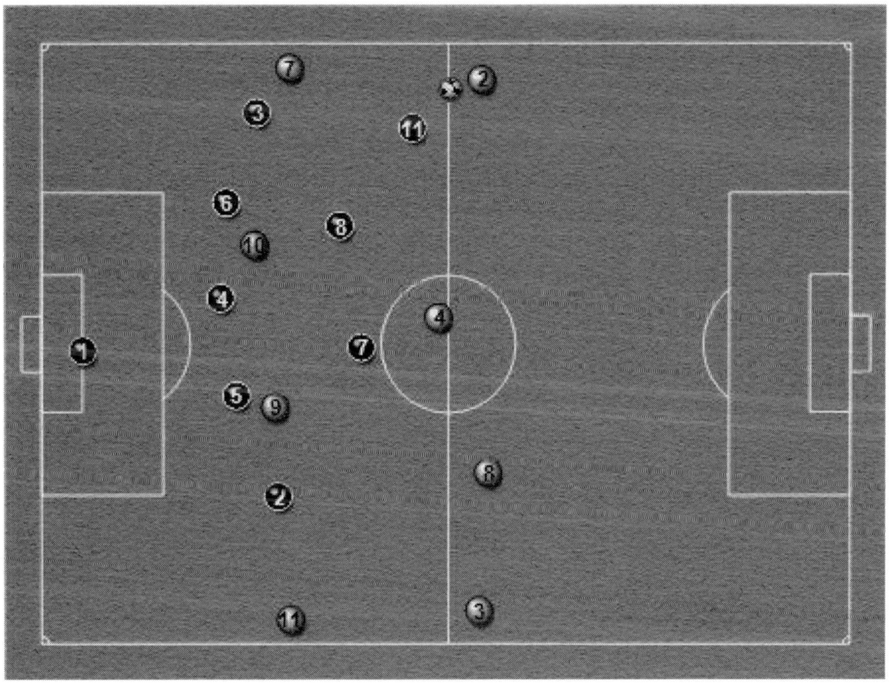

In front of these central midfielders are the 2 strikers. One of these strikers will be required to balance off the midfield unit when the ball is being switched to negate the radical movement of the central midfield as mentioned above.

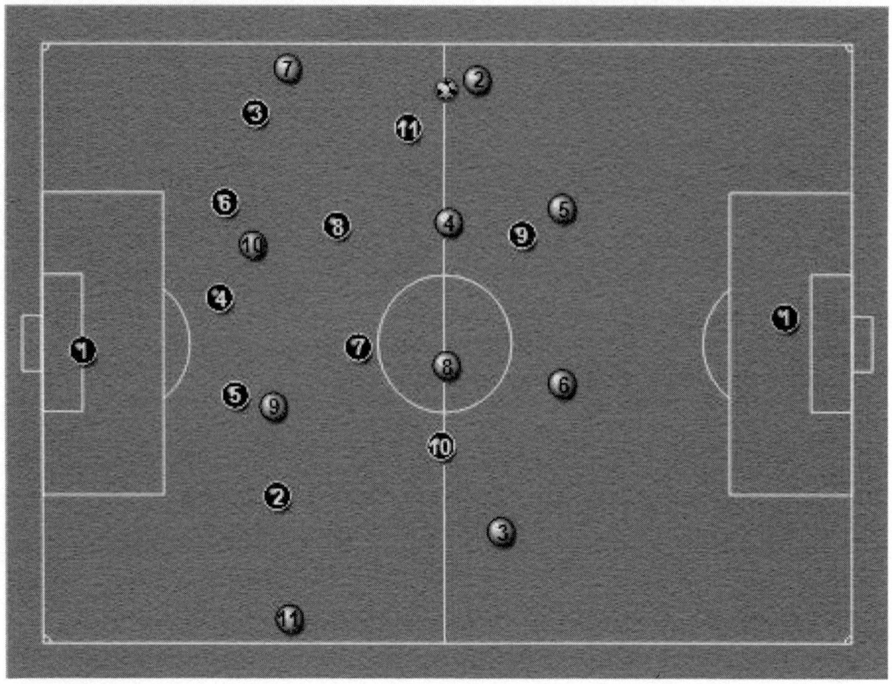

The 352 system is an offensive one as with operating with only 3 defenders it enables an extra player to advance from the back and supplement the forward actions of the team. The back 3 players, when initiating play from the back, will spread the full width of the field and try to get the central player of the 3 on the ball from where he can pass to either wide central defender, stretching the opposition immediately.

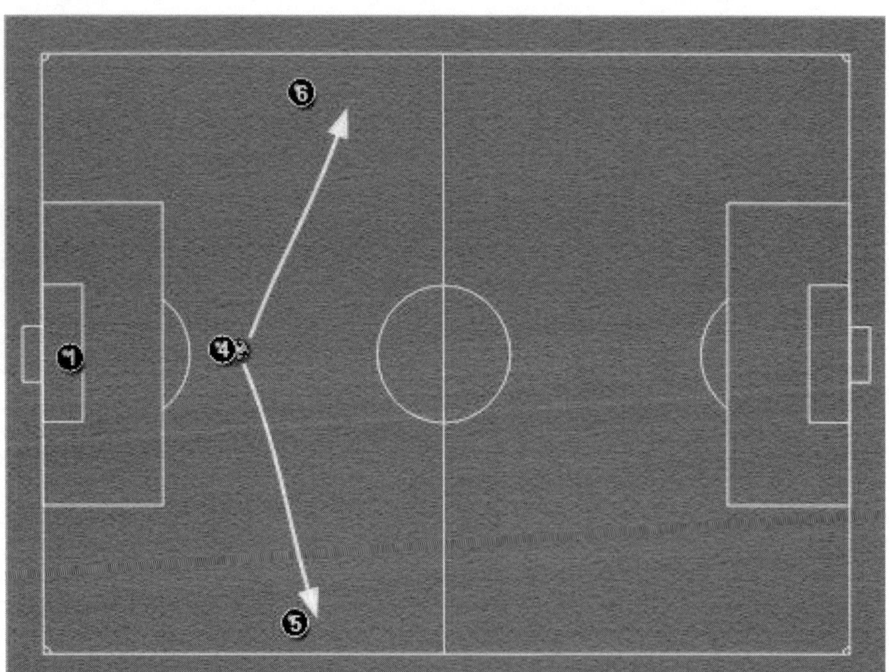

By spreading wide this pushes the wing backs up the field and enables the 352 to start to push the opposition back in an effort to begin play from the back. This is to create space for the anchor player of the midfield who they are looking to utilise as the extra man in the midfield area.

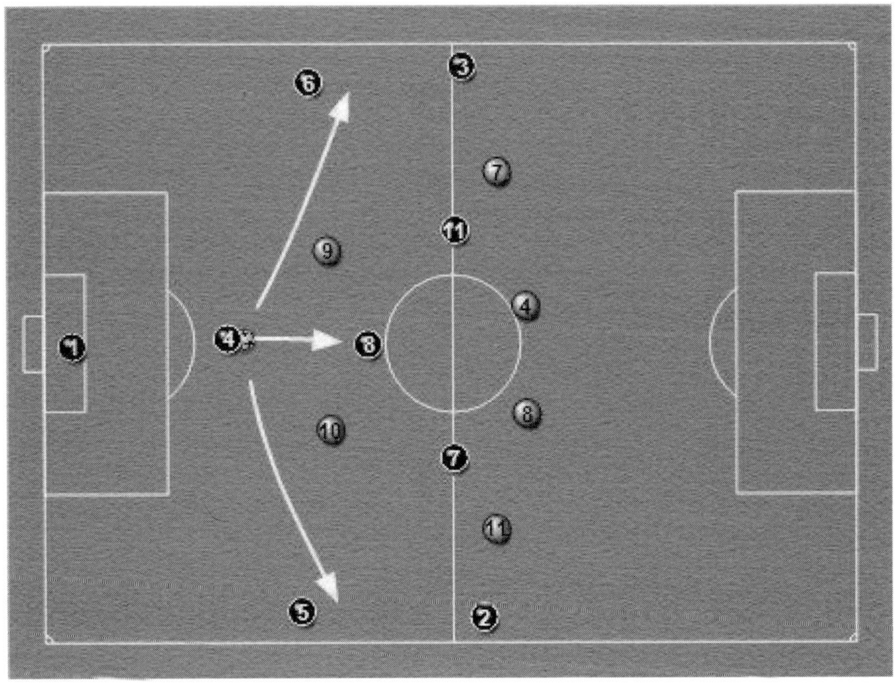

Once in the position of the anchor player being on the ball in space, the attacking options of the 352 open up considerably. If it is a striker who presses the anchor player then this opens up one of the wide centre halves again…

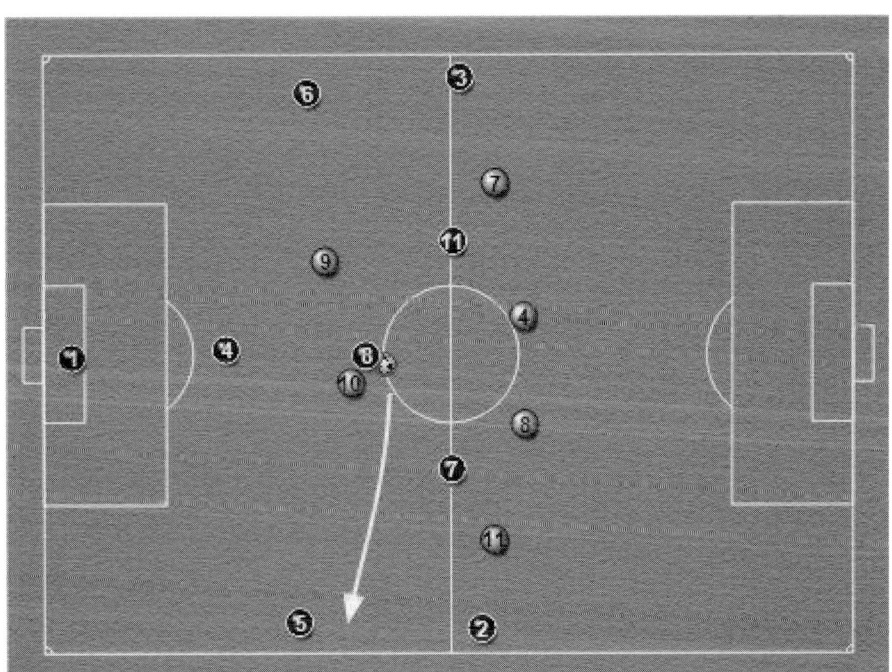

...or if a midfielder comes to meet the anchor player then a pass forward to the man he has left is available.

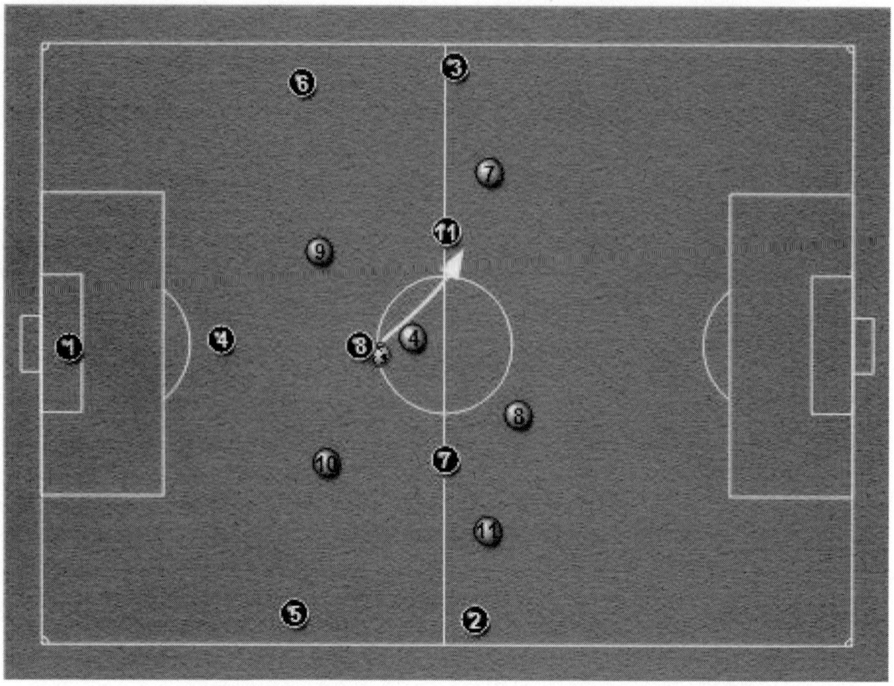

To close this gap off, if 7 comes inside to do so then this opens up the left wing back for a pass from 8.

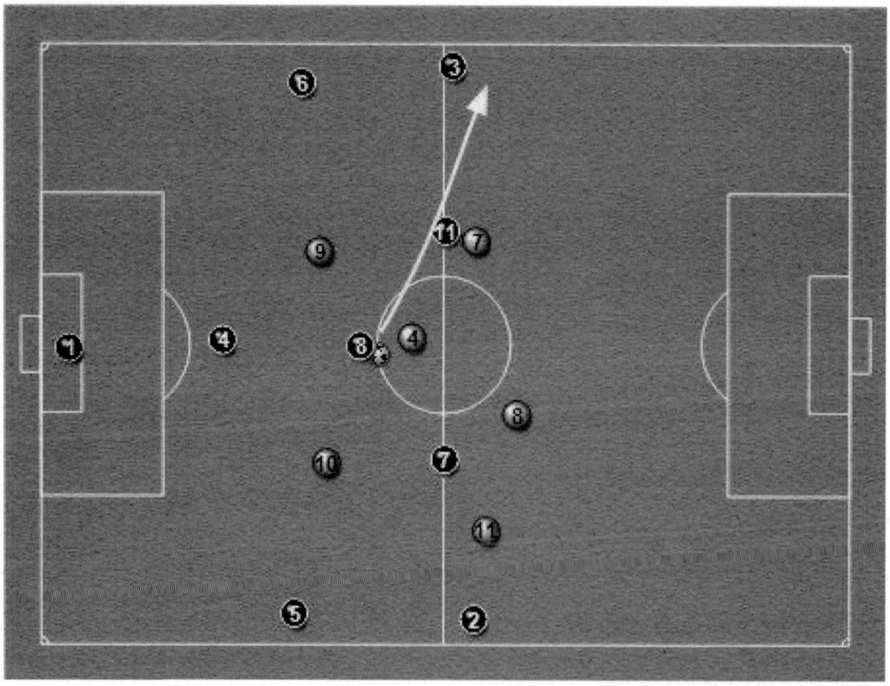

.

When we introduce the 2 strikers of the 352 the passing options of the anchor player become even more varied.

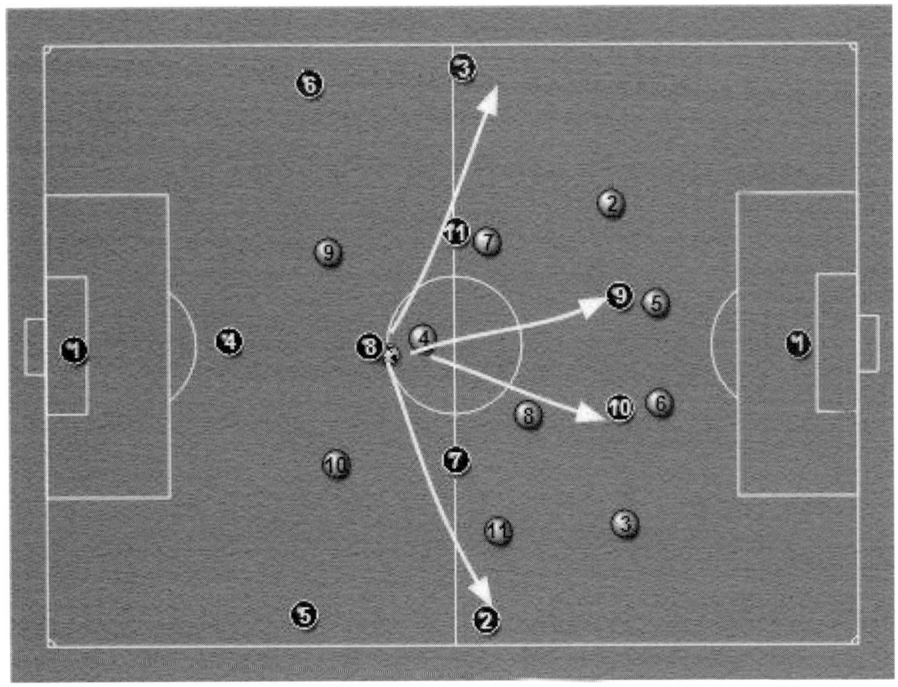

Once in wide positions the extra forward player that playing with 3 at the back creates enables a central midfielder to get into the penalty area for any cross full in the knowledge that the midfield area is well defended against any potential counter attack.

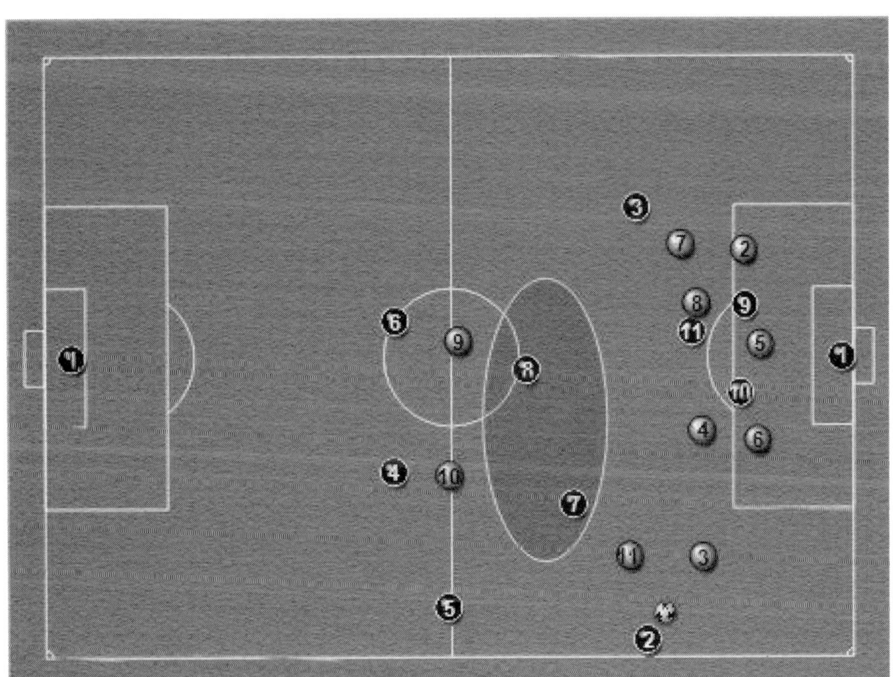

CHAPTER 2

STRENGTHS & WEAKNESSES

STRENGTHS OF THE SYSTEM

Through operating with only 3 defenders the 352 system enables an extra player to become involved with the offensive tactics of the team and thus space can be created through movement to allow a player to be free and receive the ball. The main player who benefits from this is the anchor midfield player who is often described as the playmaker. If he is allowed to be free and receive the ball then his options to pass the ball and dictate possession of the football become numerous. It is imperative that we negate the effectiveness of this player if we are to be successful in beating the 352 system.

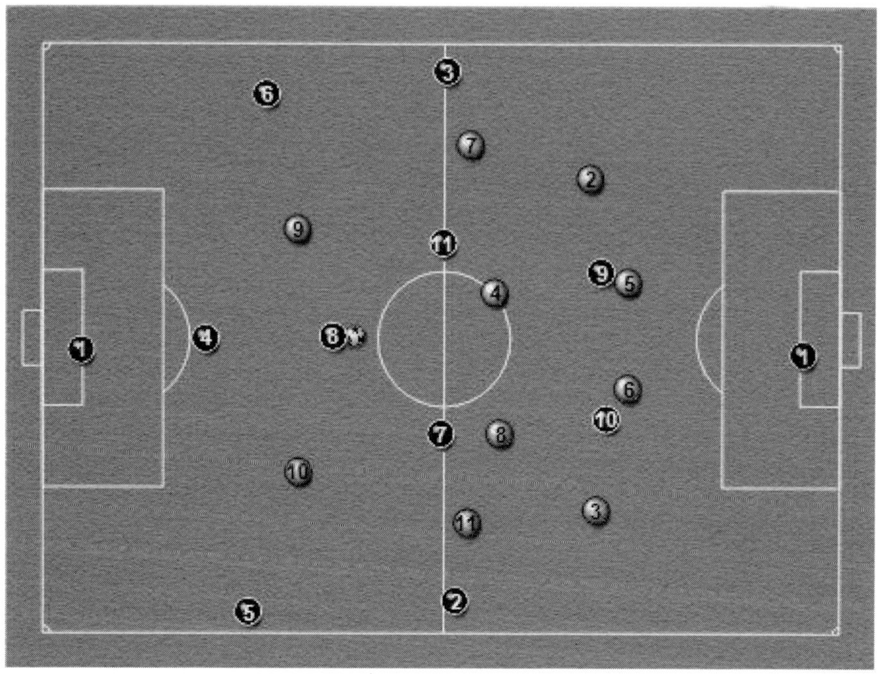

Teams find it much easier to play out from the back when operating with 3 defenders rather than 4 due to the angles created by having a player central receiving the ball. Against 2 strikers, by the wide defenders spreading themselves wide and the central player getting on the ball, long passes to players in space can be made and energy can be wasted by the front players in closing down.

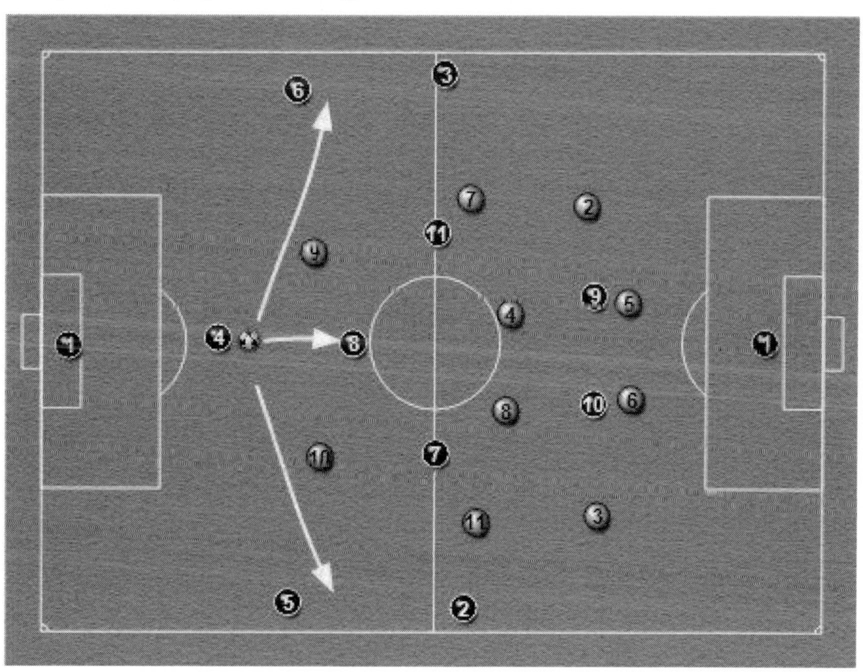

The central attacking options of the 352 system are evident as there are 3 central midfield players and 2 strikers, making 5 players in total who can support each other and form a potent central attacking force for the 352 system.

Any ball played into the strikers can be quickly supported by a central midfielder who can be adventurous in going forward secure in the knowledge that he is well covered behind him with the other 2 central midfielders.

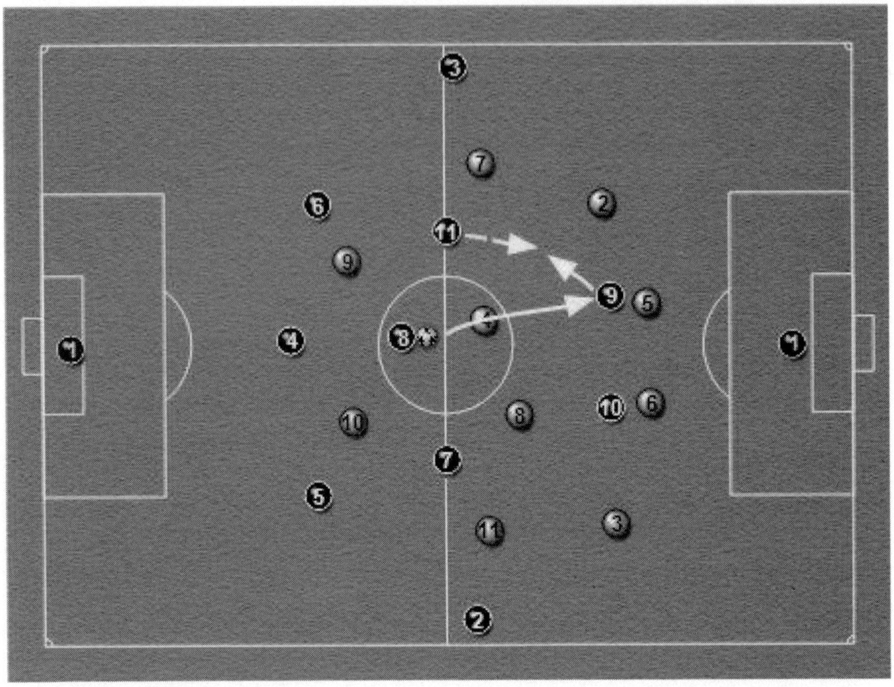

Similarly, any cross that comes into the penalty area can be attacked by a central midfielder who effectively becomes a third striker for the 352 system.

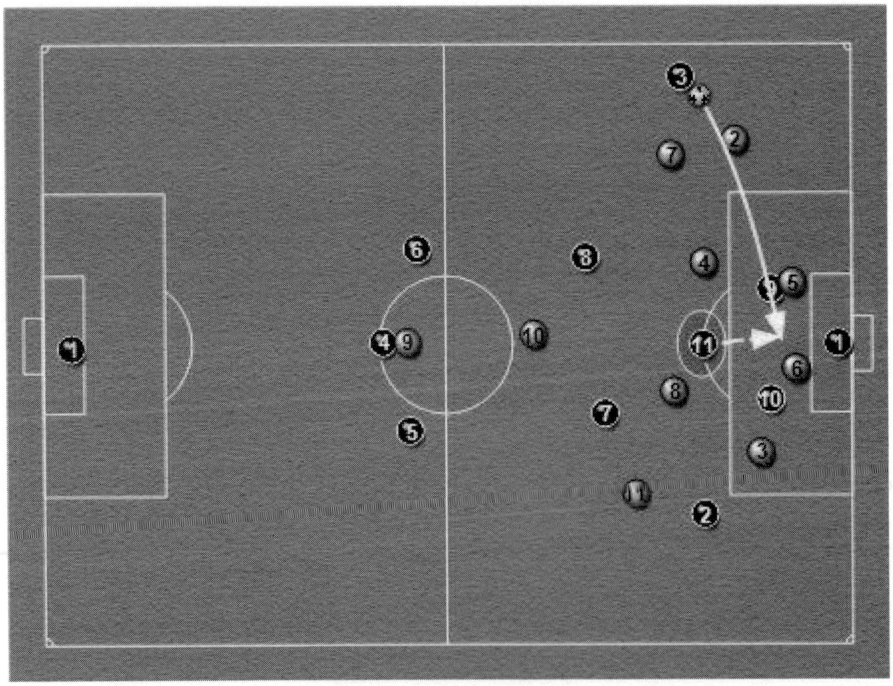

WEAKNESSES OF THE SYSTEM

One of the weaknesses of the 352 system is the inability to cover the channel areas behind its defense. With the wing backs having a great deal of offensive duties to undertake as well as being responsible for the channels of the pitch defensively, the 3 man central defense can be easily turned around so that it is retreating towards its own goal line by a simple ball played into the channel.

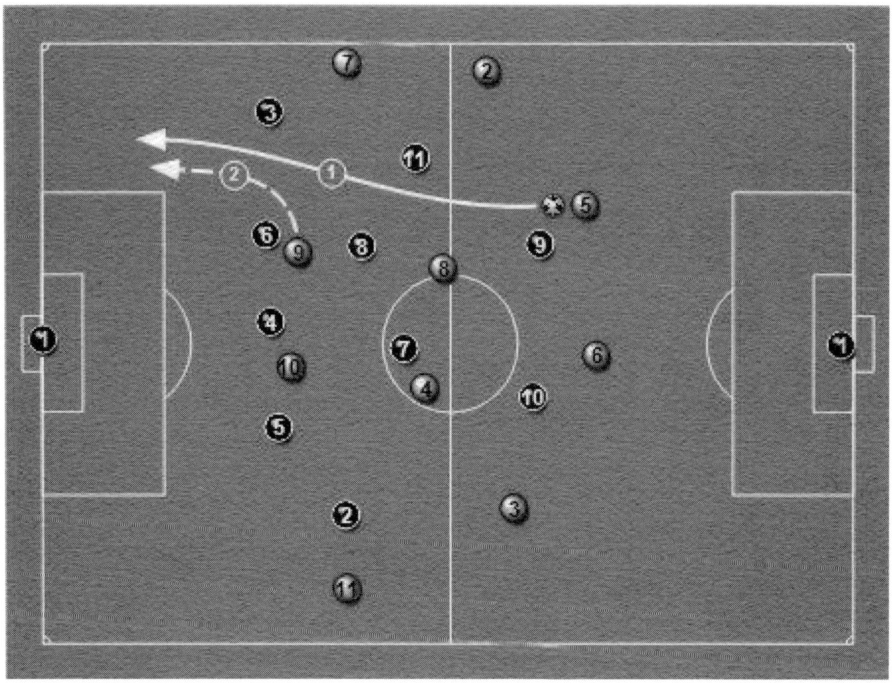

When the ball gets central and further forward, these channels become even more imperative to defend and thus the wing backs have to drop in to make sure they are less accessible. This creates a lack of players further forward to be able to deal with the opposition and therefore keeping possession of the ball becomes easier. A major flaw in the 352 system is the fact that when the ball is central it can get pegged back into a back 5.

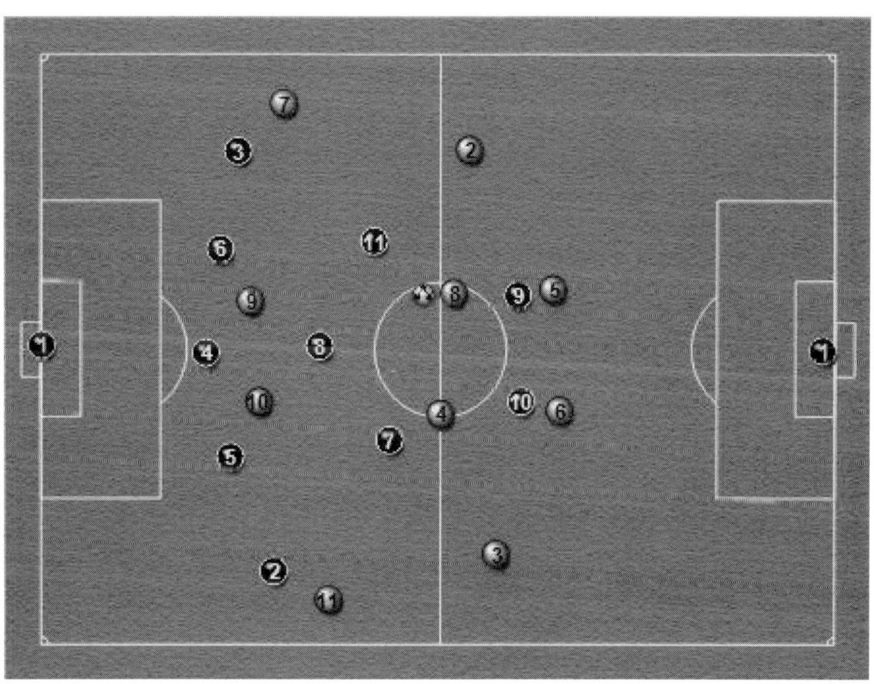

When the ball is wide against the 352 system, it is the opposite channel which becomes unguarded and a quick effective switch of the ball can often penetrate behind it.

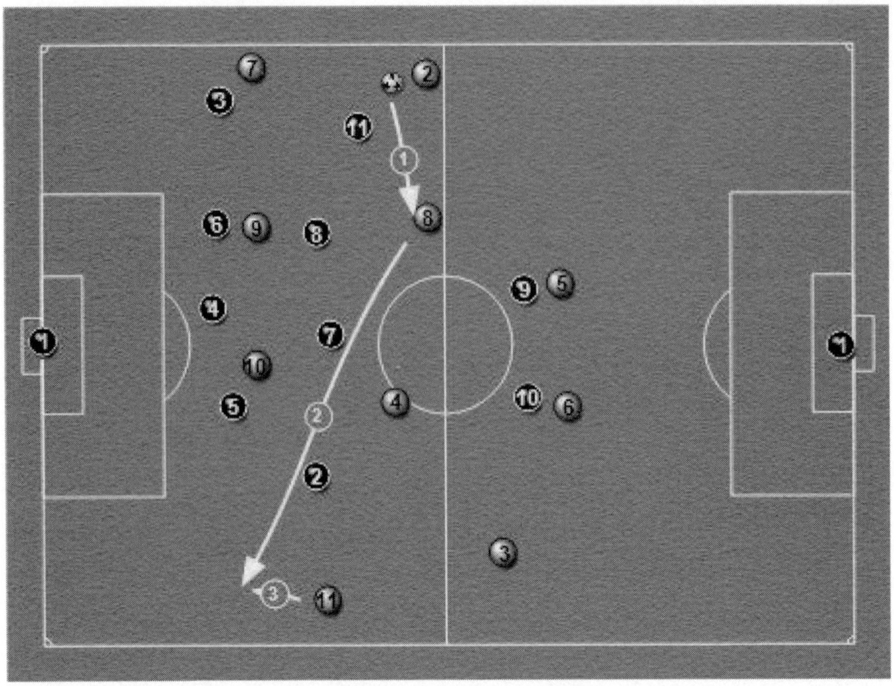

In possession, the fact that centrally the 352 system is very strong means that in wide areas it can become weak with only one player responsible for gaining width in the system. If we can meet the wing back high up the pitch, in order for him to gain support and not be crowded out, elaborate movement to overlap and support has to be effected by the 352 system which can lead to confusion and a lack of defensive positioning should they lose the ball.

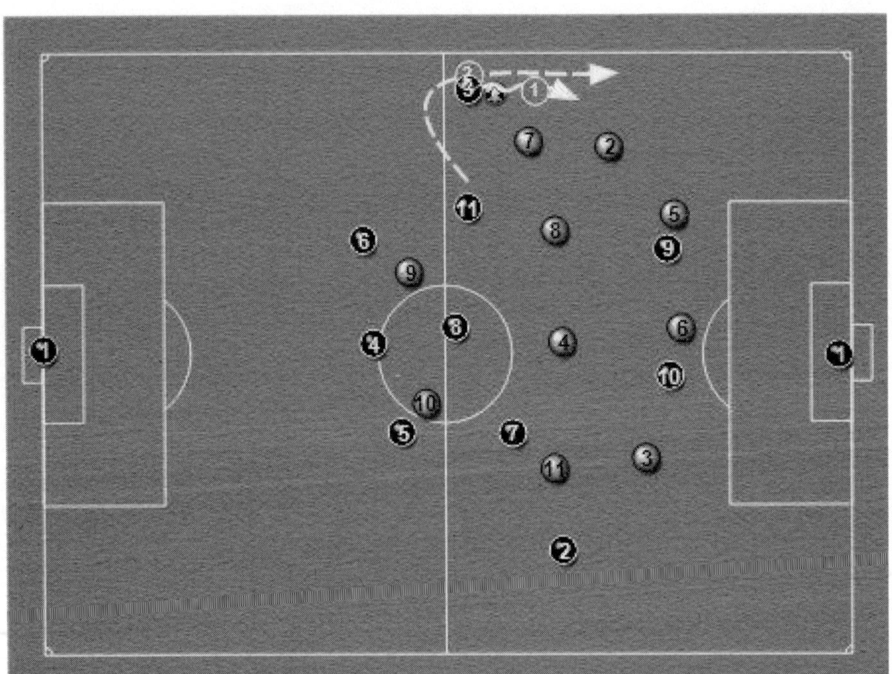

CHAPTER 3

DEFENDING AGAINST THE 3-5-2

Attacking Third

The defensive shape I have chosen for us to occupy is a 4-3-3 system, and this needs to drop into more of a 4-5-1 formation when the ball is with the goalkeeper of the 352 in the attacking third. This makes us compact enough to deal with the potential ball played long direct from the goalkeeper. It will encourage the 352 to initiate play from the back where we can then begin to start our press.

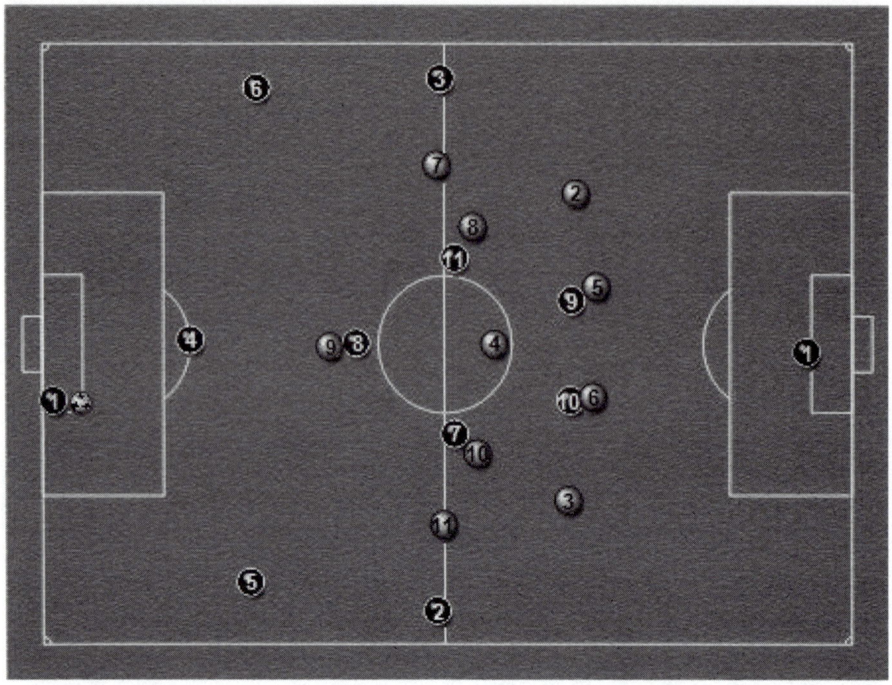

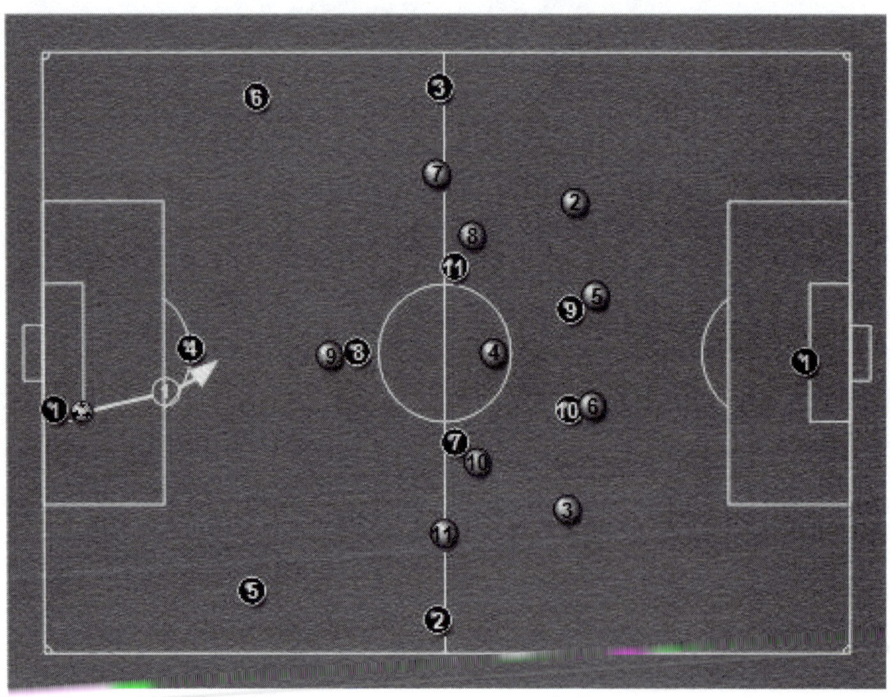

By allowing 4 to have the ball and not press him, we can remain very compact in the central part of the field which encourages him to pass to one of the wide centre halves.

As the ball is travelling from 4 out to 6 as in this instance our players must move accordingly in order to make sure that a high press is initiated.

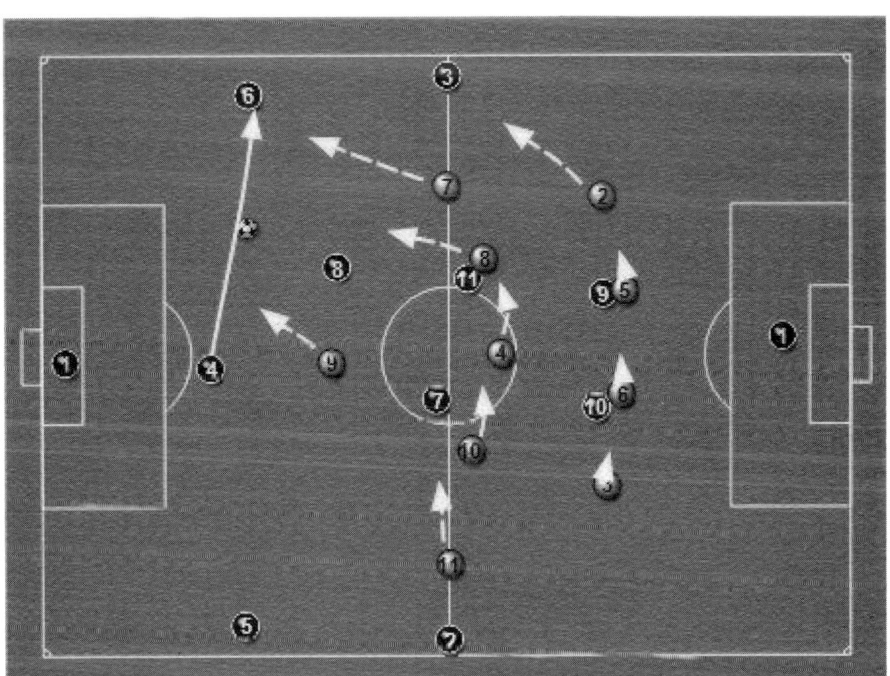

This high press encourages a high tempo game which makes the 352 play in a more predictable manner enabling us to take more of the initiative even when the 352 has the ball. Here 9 has closed won the potential pass back to 4, 8 has stepped out of the midfield area to negate any pass inside to their 8 and to compensate for this movement, the other 2 midfield players, 4 & 10 have shuffled across accordingly. 11, our left winger, takes up a half and half position where he balances off the team shape. The back 4, as the ball has been travelling, shuffle across and mark zonally with the right full back, 2, pushing high onto their 3 which is going to be the least dangerous pass that their 6 can make due to our 7 closing down in a manner which encourages play towards the touchline.

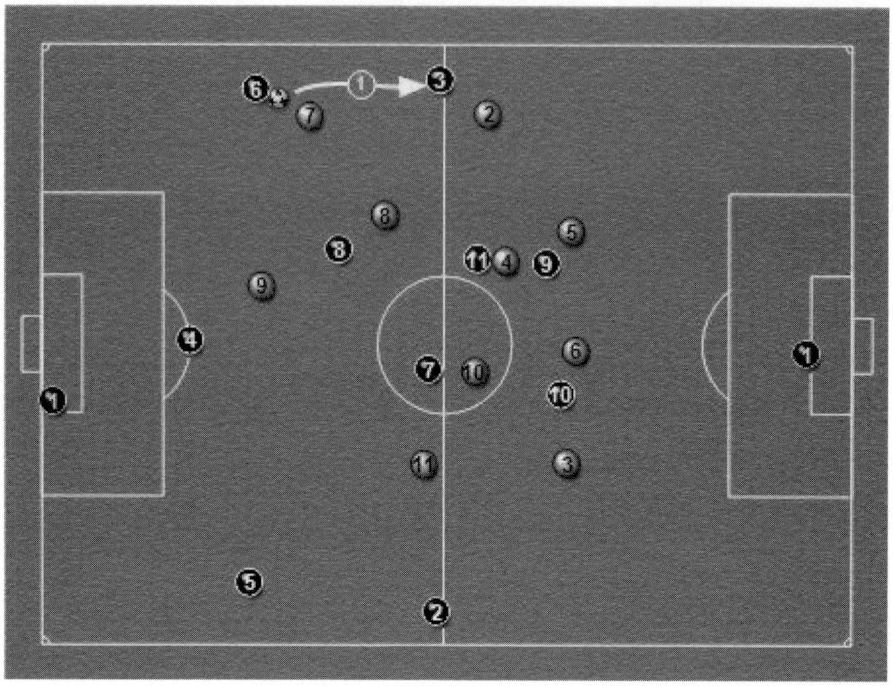

If 2 is quick enough and the pass is made in a hurry he can try and intercept the pass from where we can initiate a counter attack.

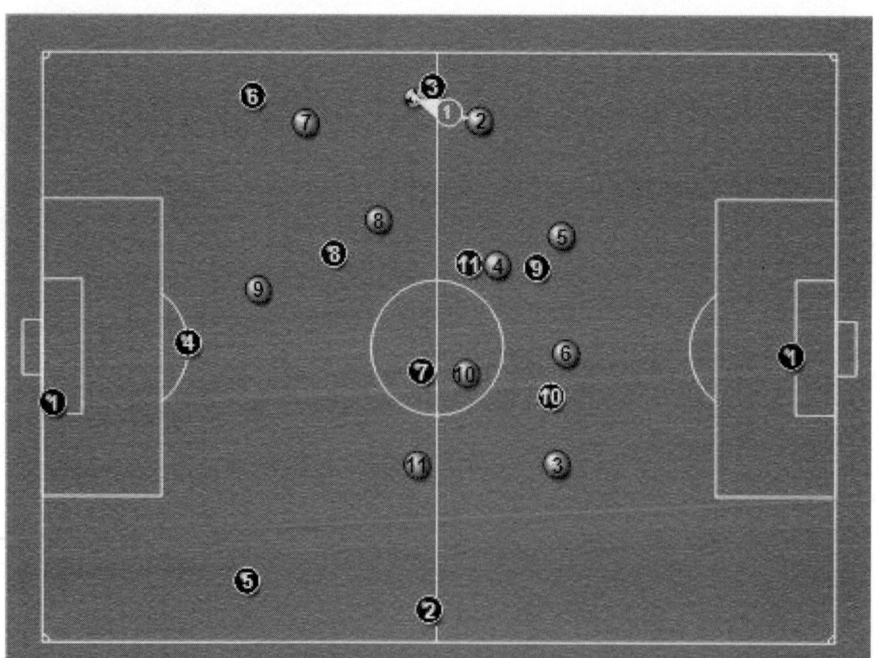

Obviously the players of the 352 system may be good enough to manipulate the ball into the anchor player (8) who may then switch the ball to the other side.

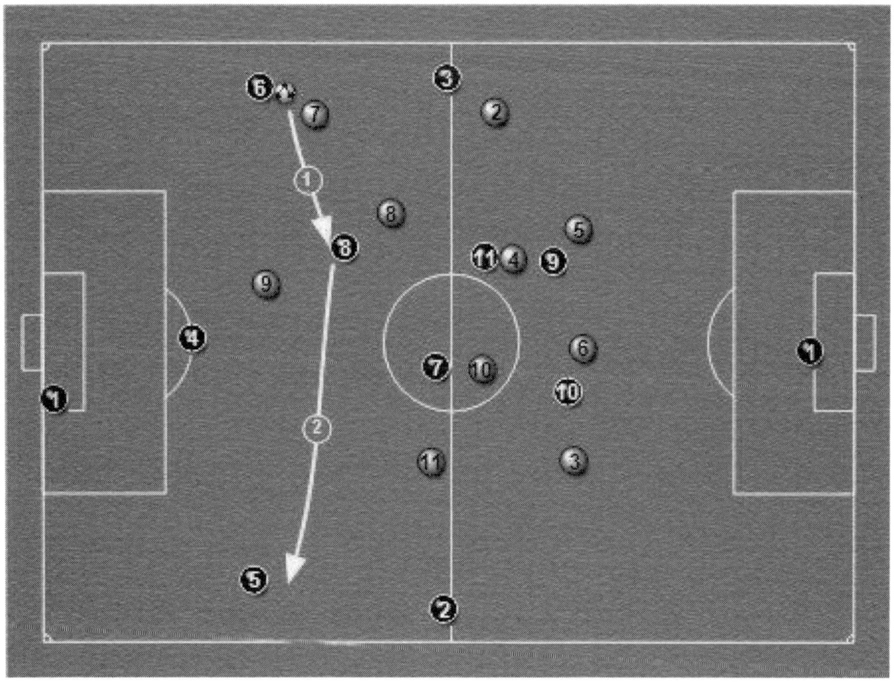

If the switch that is effected by the 352 is slow and not threatening to us, ie; they play backwards of square, our whole team can shuffle across accordingly to mirror the tactic used initially on closing the ball down.

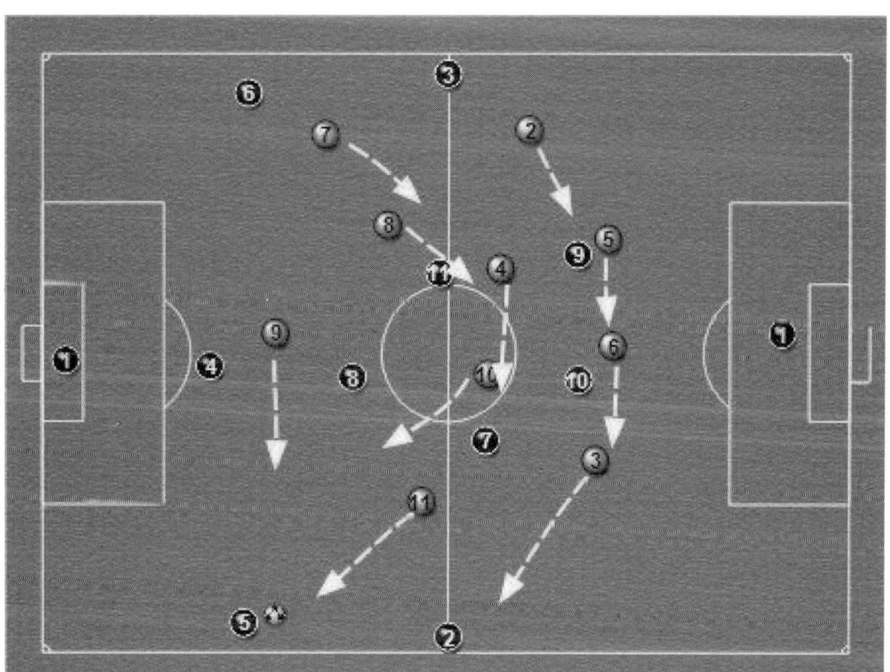

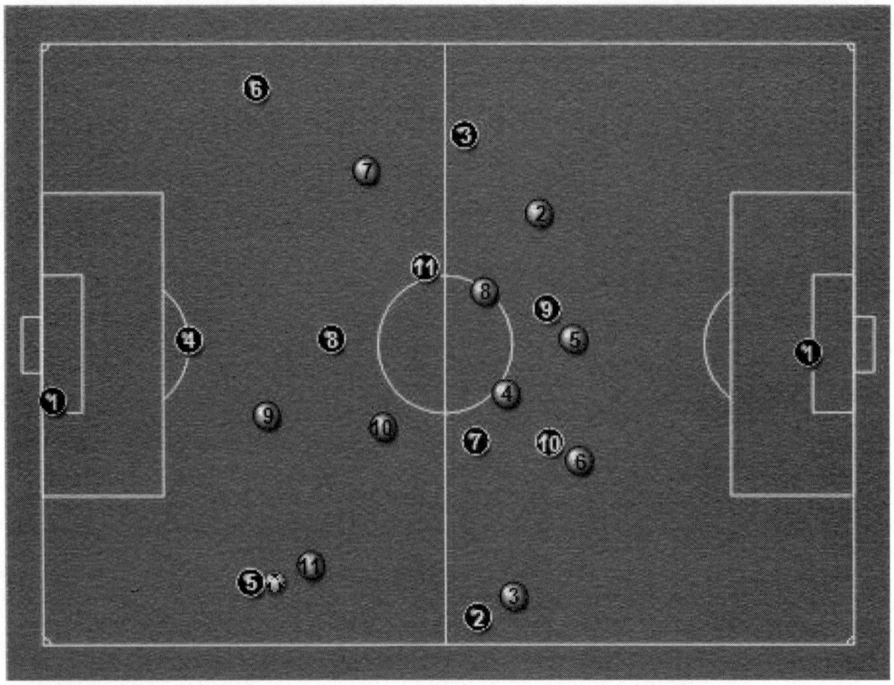

If the switch that is effected by the 352 is a more positive one and the ball is passed forward of square then we need to recognise the danger of this….

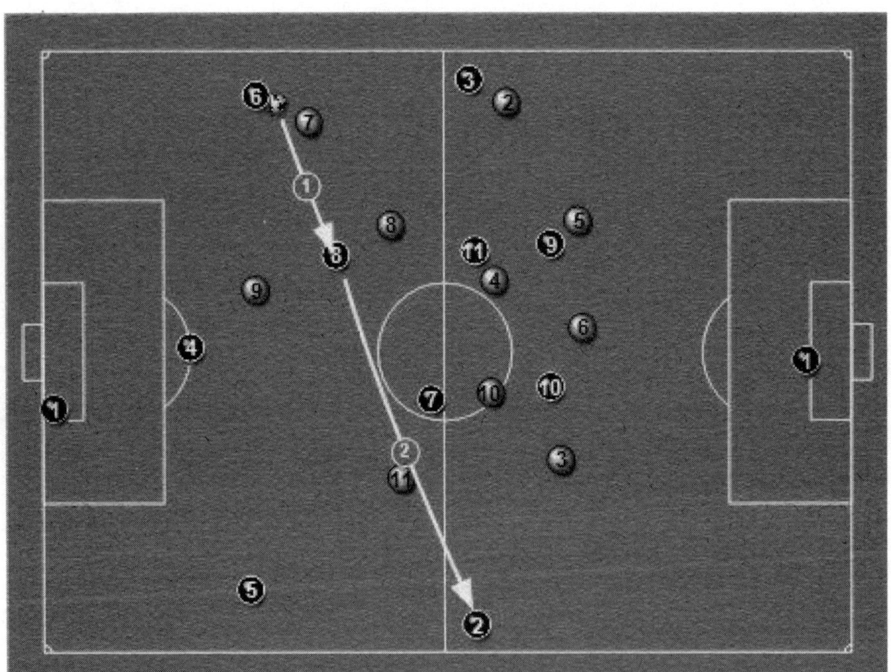

...and as the ball is travelling we need to retreat accordingly to take care of the situation and retain the compact nature of our units.

Once in this position we need to start to effect our Mid Third defending.

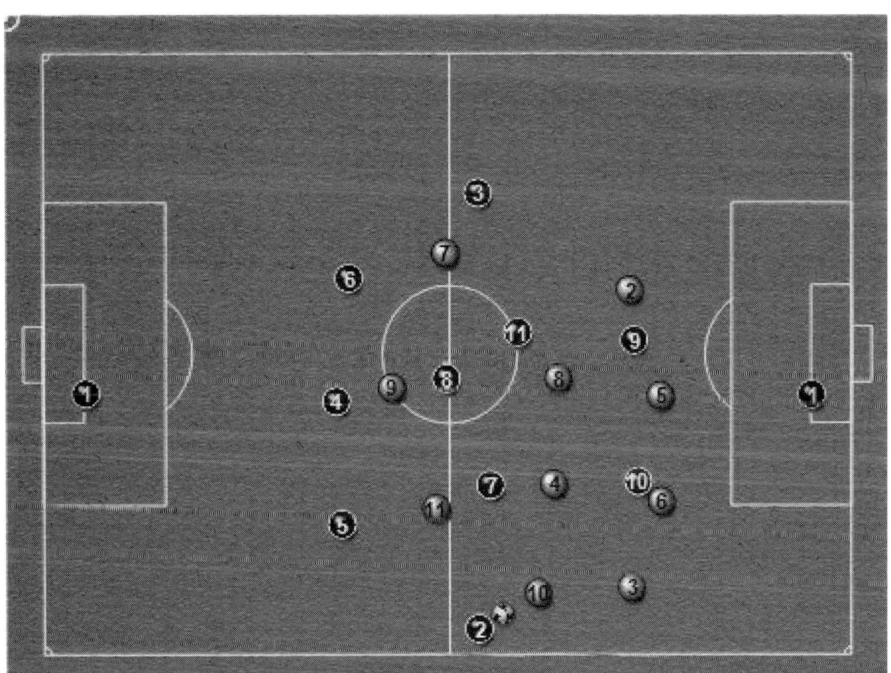

CHAPTER 4

Practices for Defending in the Attacking Third

1

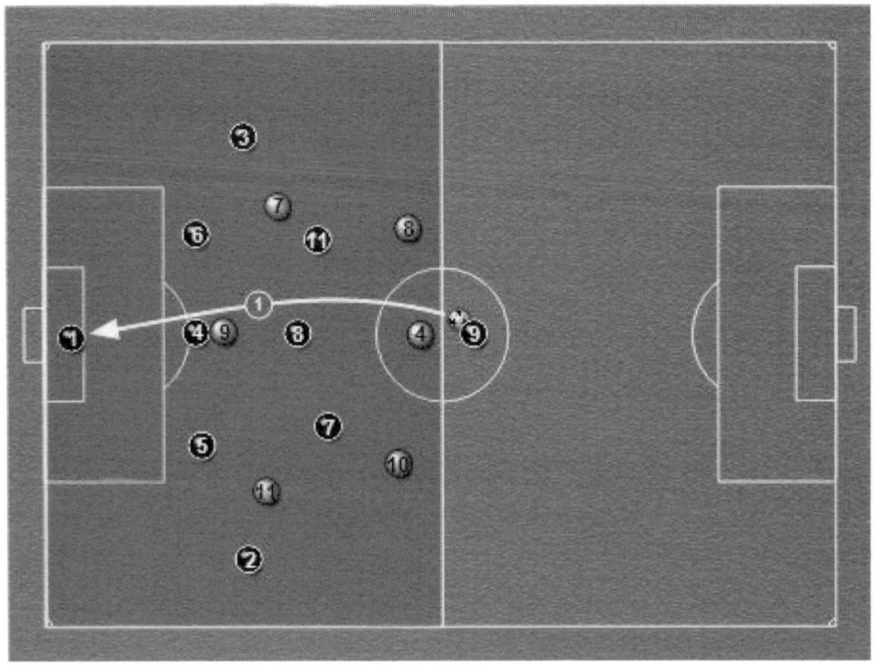

Start as shown.
Objective is to make sure that the ball is transferred wide initially and then stays there.
Defending team scores by getting the ball into 9.

2

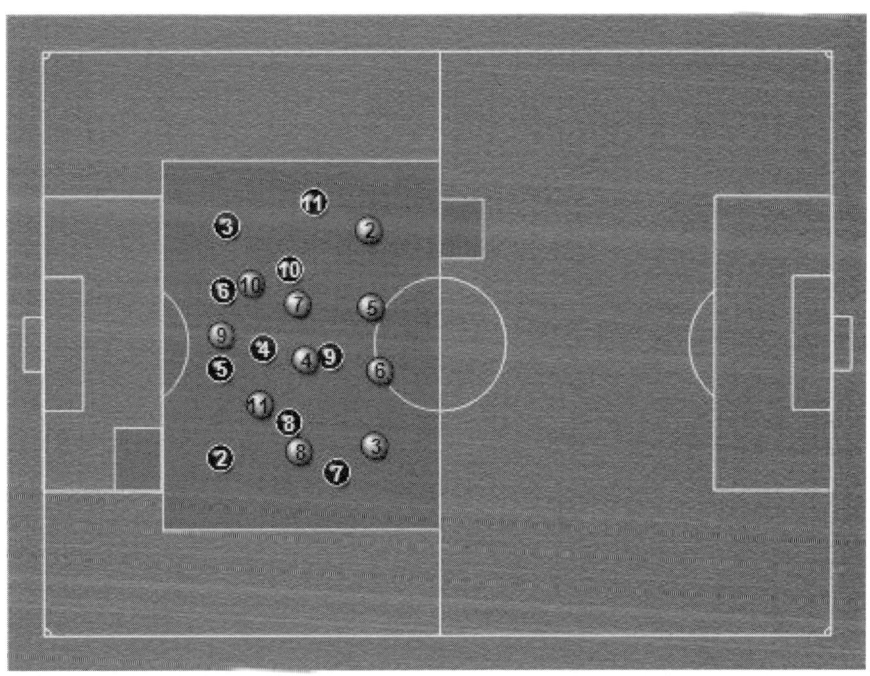

As a warm up split the players into equal teams and play in team formation if numbers permit.
Players transfer the ball to each other via their hands and are not allowed to run with the ball.
The ball can be only be won through interception.

3

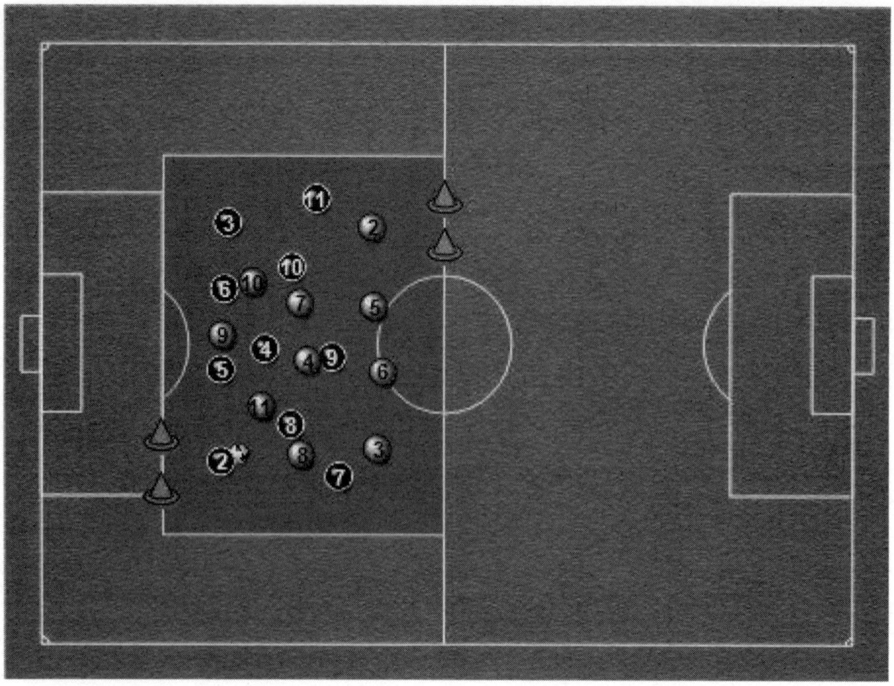

Progress to the same drill but playing normal football.
The objective is to score in the goal.

4

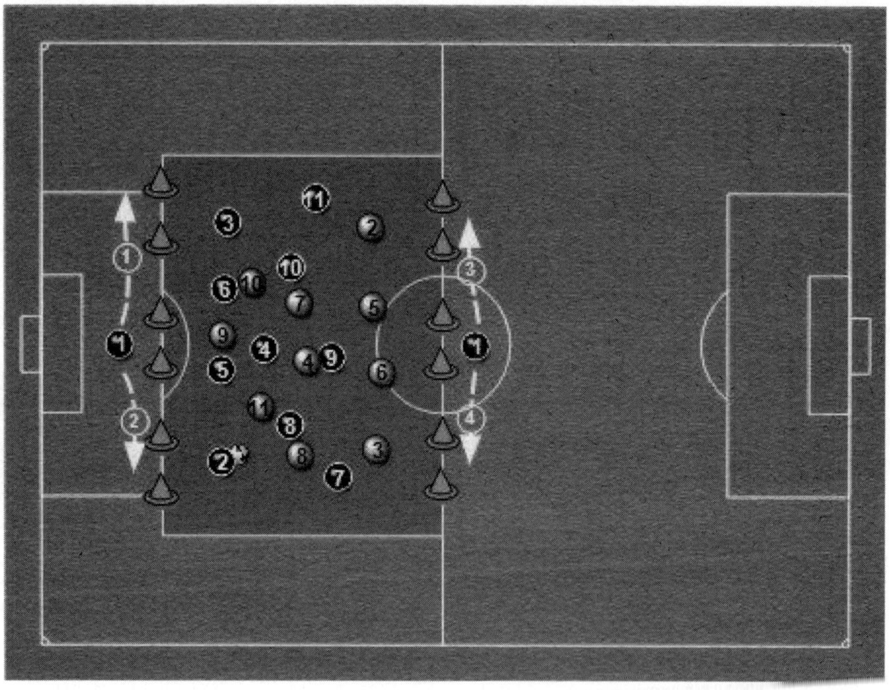

Set up the drill as shown with the cones being circa 3 yards apart for each goal.
The objective is to score in a goal which is not defended by the Goalkeeper.
Cannot score in a goal defended by the goalkeeper.

CHAPTER 5

DEFENDING AGAINST THE 3-5-2

Mid Third

The central midfield 3 have to be very hard working as they must cover the whole width of the field, leaving the 2 wingers to be bale to operate in the offensive part of the field as much as is possible. Here the left sided central midfield player, 10, has shuffled across and continues to attempt to force the play outside towards the touchline, in the knowledge that one of the strengths of the 352 is its central attacking propensity. 10's position should be such that if a straight line was drawn from the ball through his body it would continue goal-wards and dissect the near post of the goal. With the central midfielders shuffling all the way across to defend the situation, it is important that the weak side winger, 7, balances the team off by dropping deeper into a half and half position, from where he can help out if needed but if the ball is won he is well positioned to join in the counter attack. The left side winger, 11, pulls into a wide position in an effort to disturb the 3 man central defensive unit of the 352.

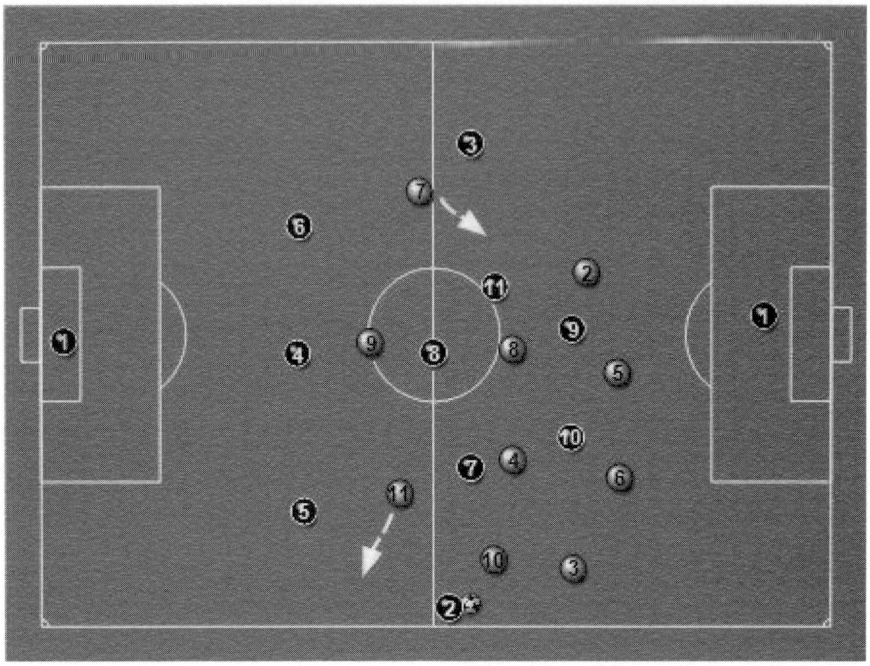

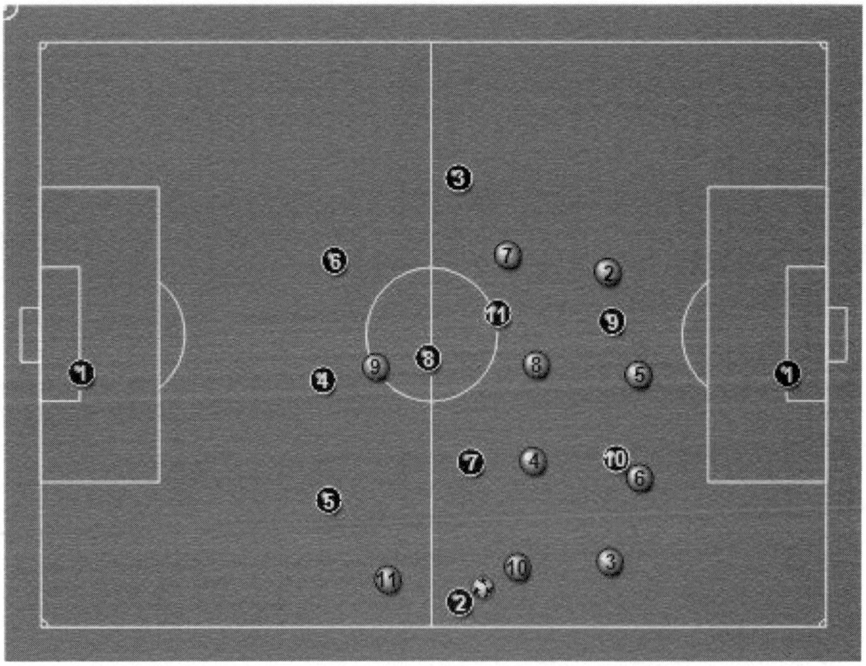

As we stated in the Strengths & Weaknesses Chapter, in order to support the wing back when the ball is in wide positions, elaborate movement from inside to out is needed. One of the features of the 352 is the overlap of the wing back by the inside central midfielder, 7, whose movement is designed to not only provide an option for the wing back on the ball, 2, but also to create the space inside for the anchor player, 8, to get on the ball. The importance of our 3 to retain his zonal shape in line with the other defenders is fundamental in negating this type of movement from making us lose our shape.

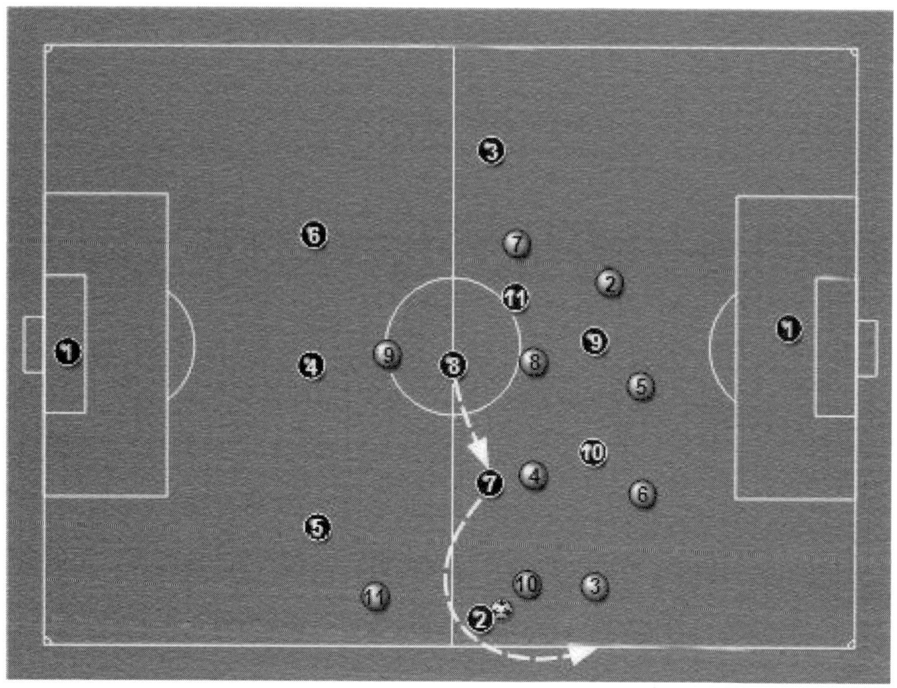

By retaining this zonal unit, our 3 can accept the run of 7 and if the position of our 10 is correct to show outside then the only easy pass possible is the ball down the touchline for 7 who has made the run.

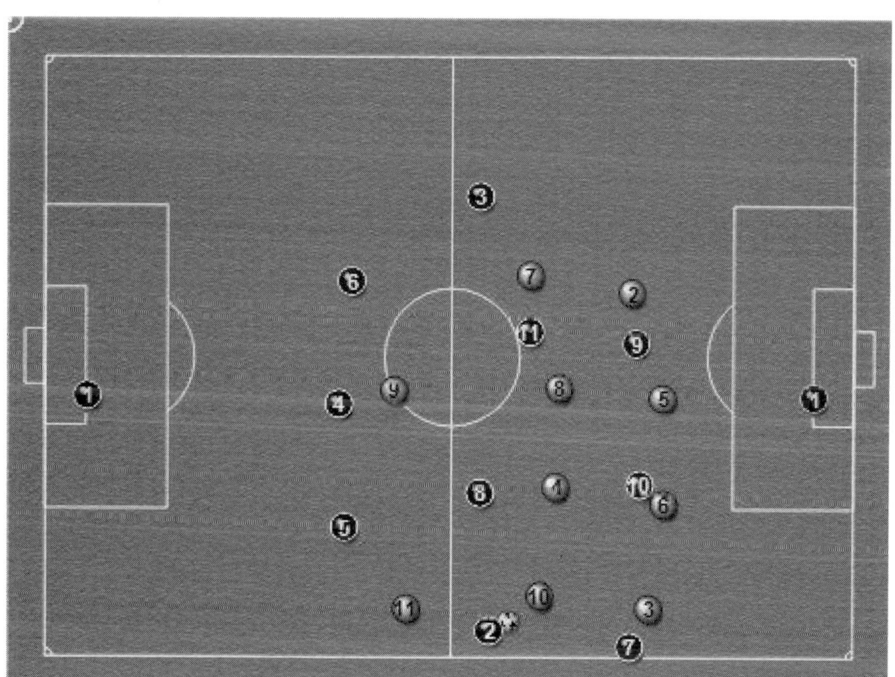

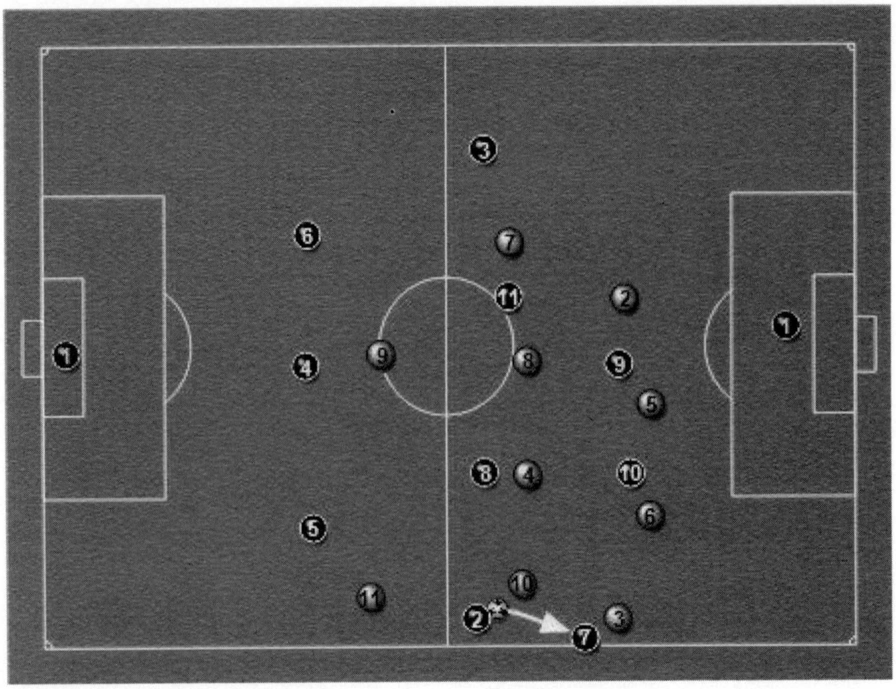

It may be possible for 3 to intercept the ball as it is played down the touchline to 7 and he should be coached to do this.

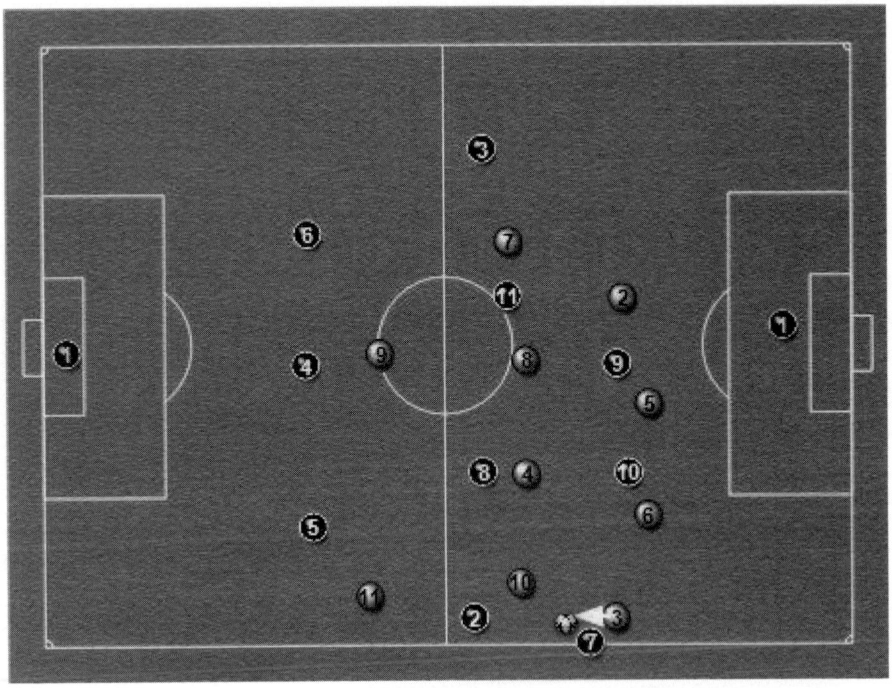

If successful there are several options open to him to set up a potential counter attack.

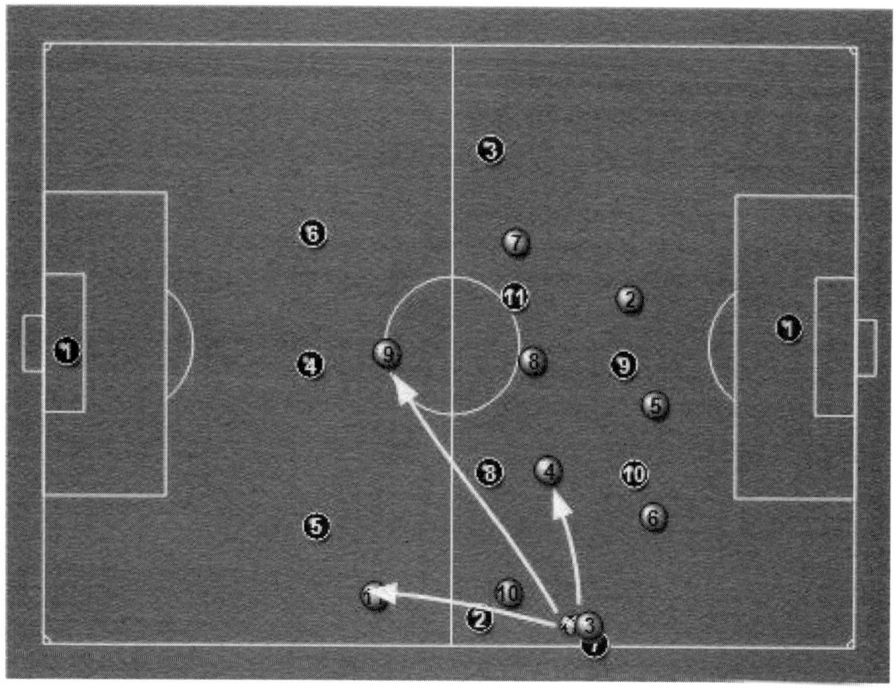

Again we must cater for us not being successful in forcing the 352 to pass down the touchline and a pass could be effected inside to the anchor player. It is important that our own anchor player, 4, does not retreat to deep in an effort to screen the back 4 as he is the player who is best placed to press their 8 as and when the ball is transferred inside.

If 4 is close enough to be able to challenge 8 and win the ball then the counterattack opportunity is on for him to drive forward with the ball which will force the 3 central defenders of the 352 to retreat and enable the 2 forward players of our system, 9 & 11, to make support this forward drive.

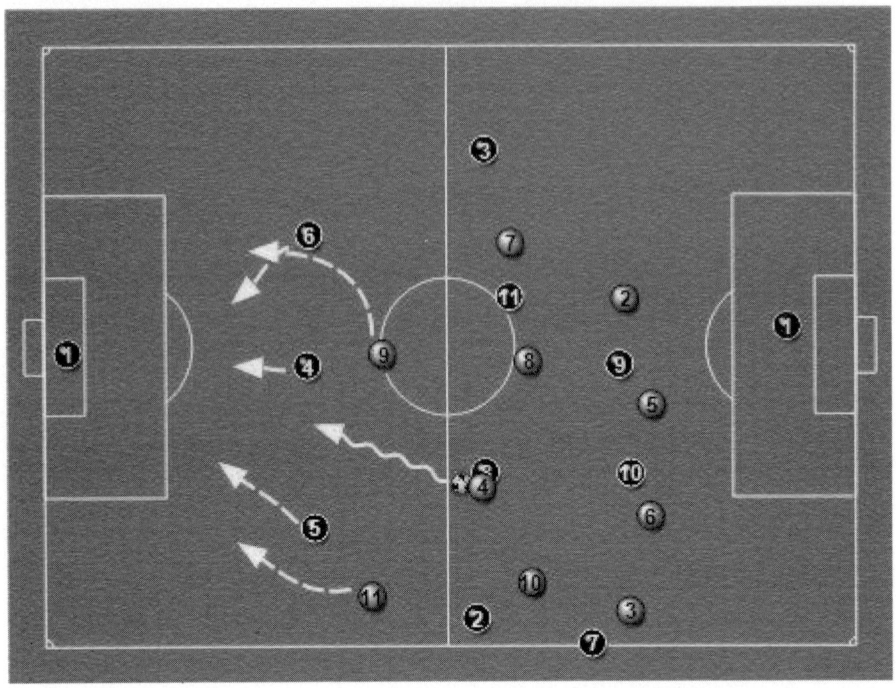

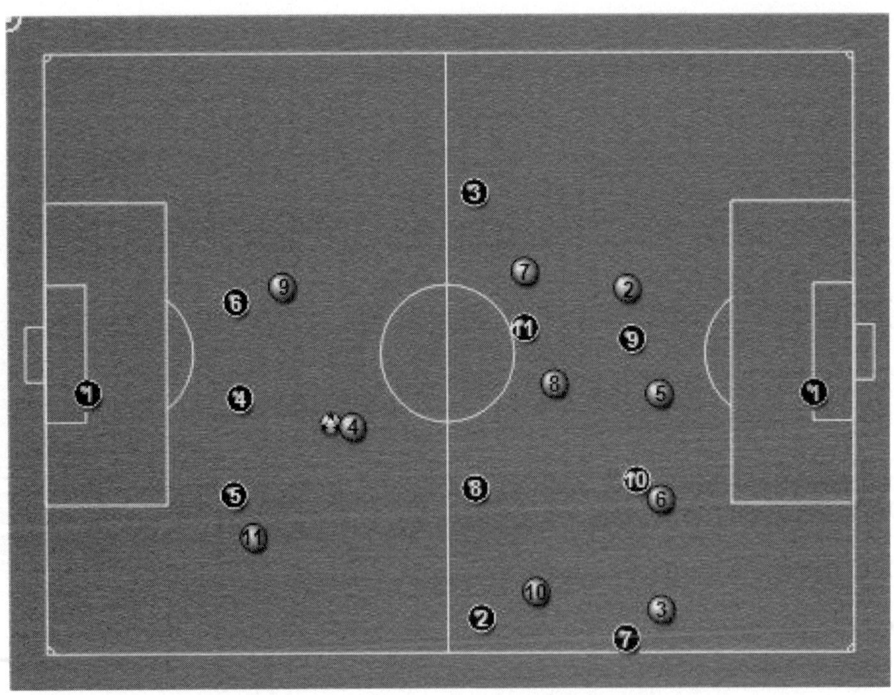

If 4 is not successful in winning the ball from 8 when it is transferred inside then it is highly likely that the ball will be switched to the other side behind our midfield line.

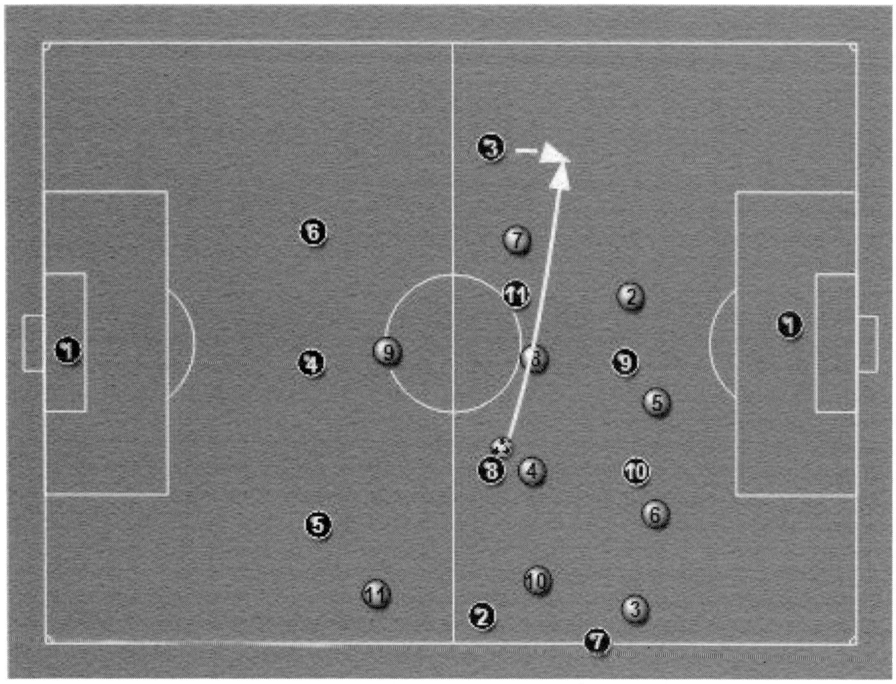

If this happens then the following scenario unfolds form where we have to look to defend in our defending third.

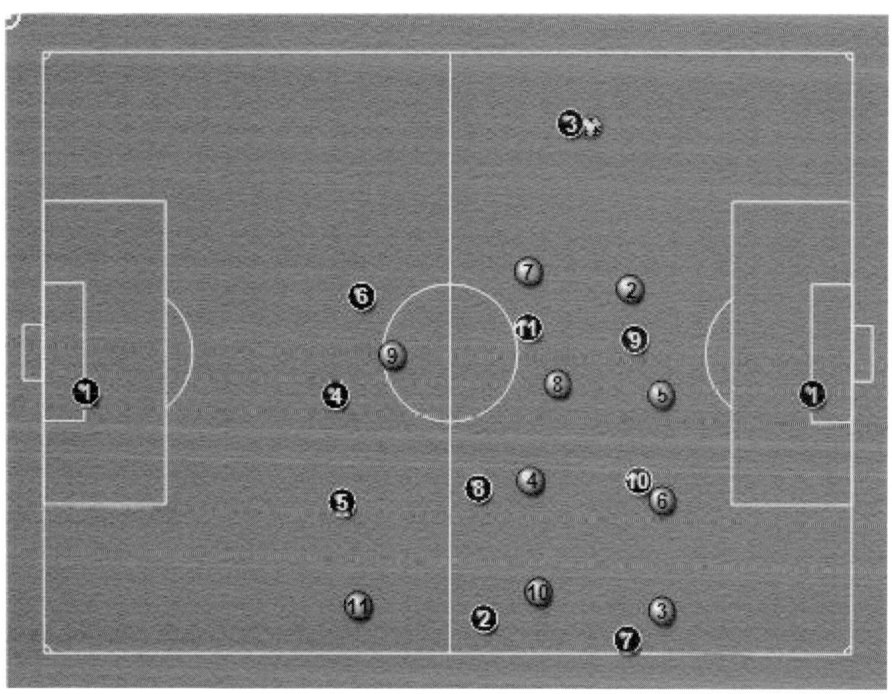

CHAPTER 6

Practices for Defending in the Mid Third

1

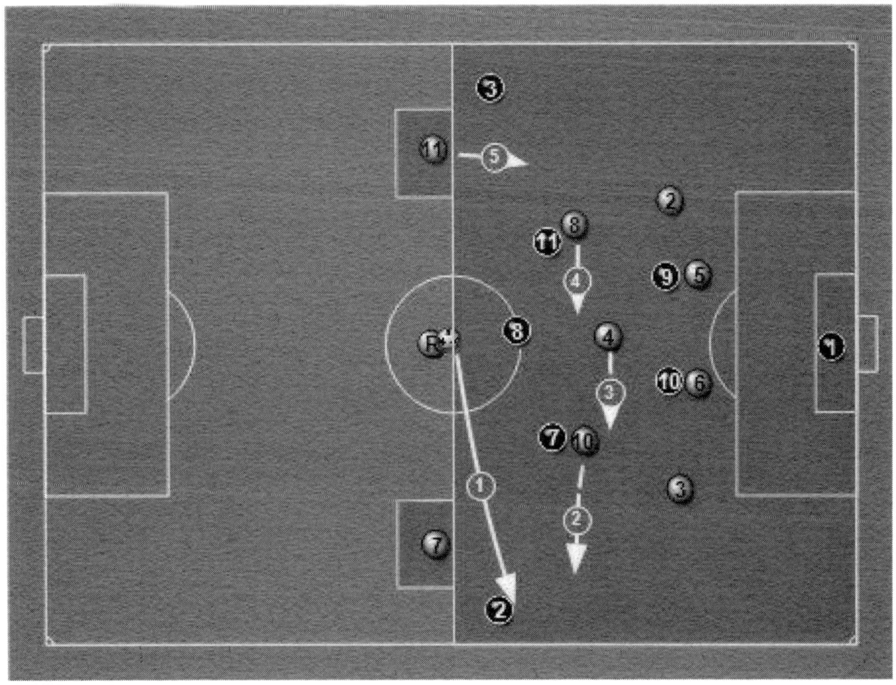

Start as shown.
Whichever side the ball goes the opposite winger drops in to balance off the team.
To score, win the ball and pass to winger in box outside of pitch.

2

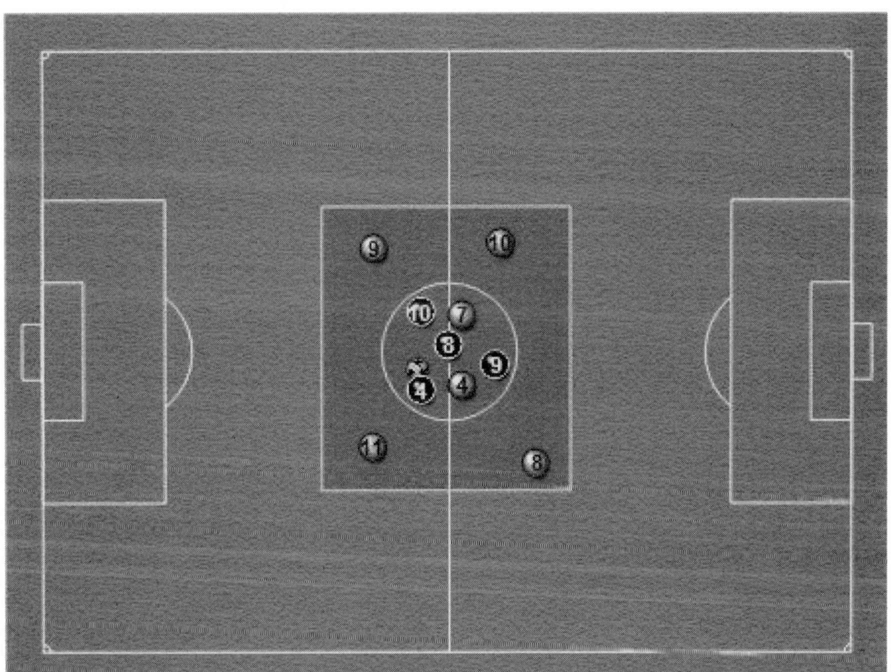

This is a counter attacking drill to coach the attitude of countering.
Play 4 v 2 in the centre circle.
When the 2 win the ball they transfer it out into the big square and play 6 v 4.
If the 4 then win the ball they transfer back to the centre circle to play 4 v 2 again.

3

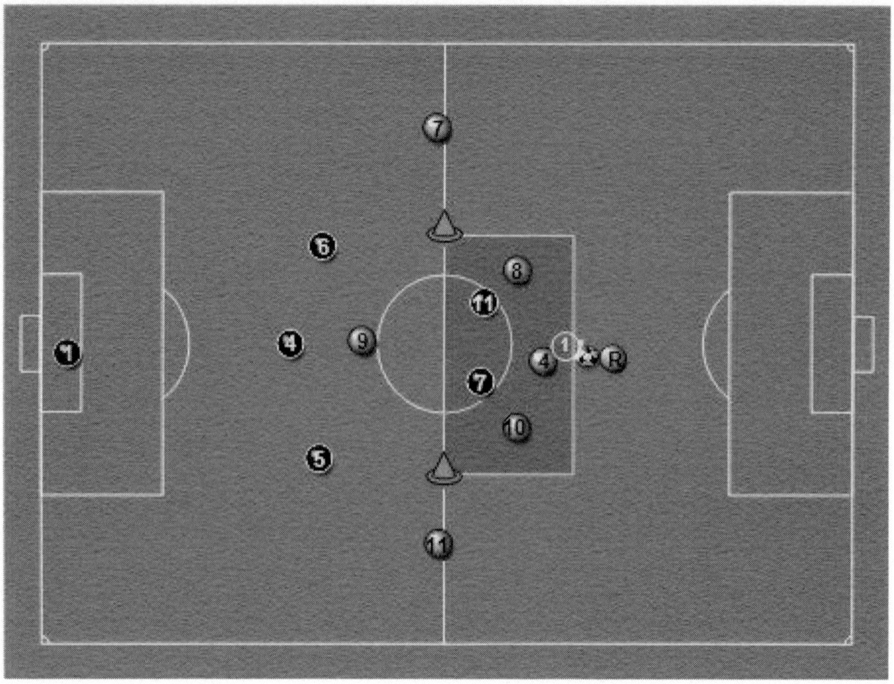

Play 3 v 2 in an area as shown.
Start as shown.
Objective is for one player from team of 3 to break the line and then attack 4 v 3 using 7, 9 & 11.

CHAPTER 7

DEFENDING AGAINST THE 3-5-2

Defending Third

The main priority when defending in the final third is to make sure that all the opponents are well marked and there is sufficient cover provided to each other. Here, as the left wing back in the 352, 2, has received the ball and travelled, it is the job of the right full back, 2, to go and challenge him and the cover is provided by the right sided midfielder, 8, leaving the right winger, 7, to sit in a hole ready to counter attack when the ball si won.

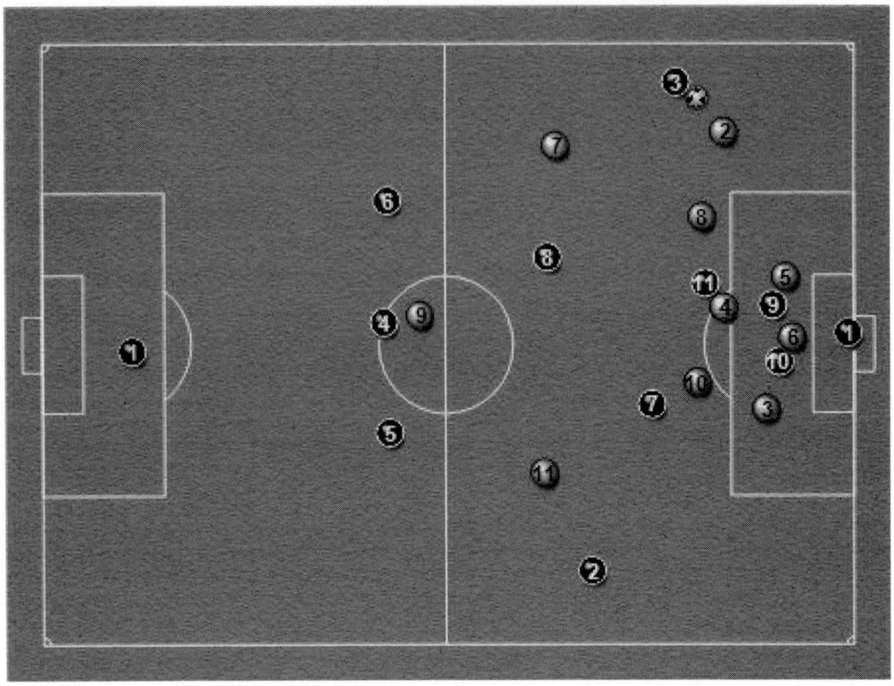

If the left wing back, 3, takes the man on and beats him, 8 is in a good position to be able to cover him and avoid him having a free run into the penalty area.

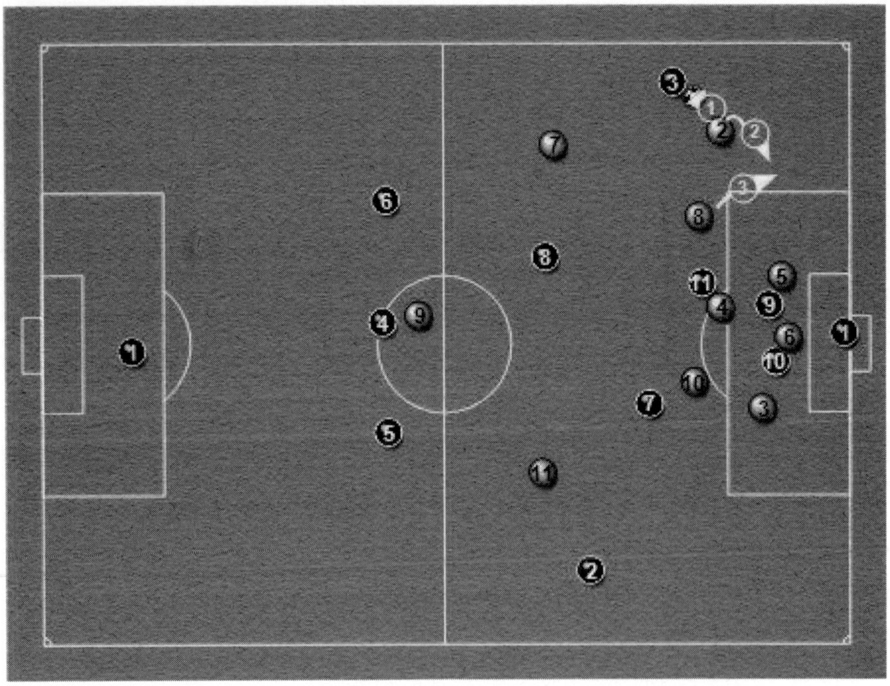

If the ball is passed back to the anchor player, 8, then he needs to be pressed...

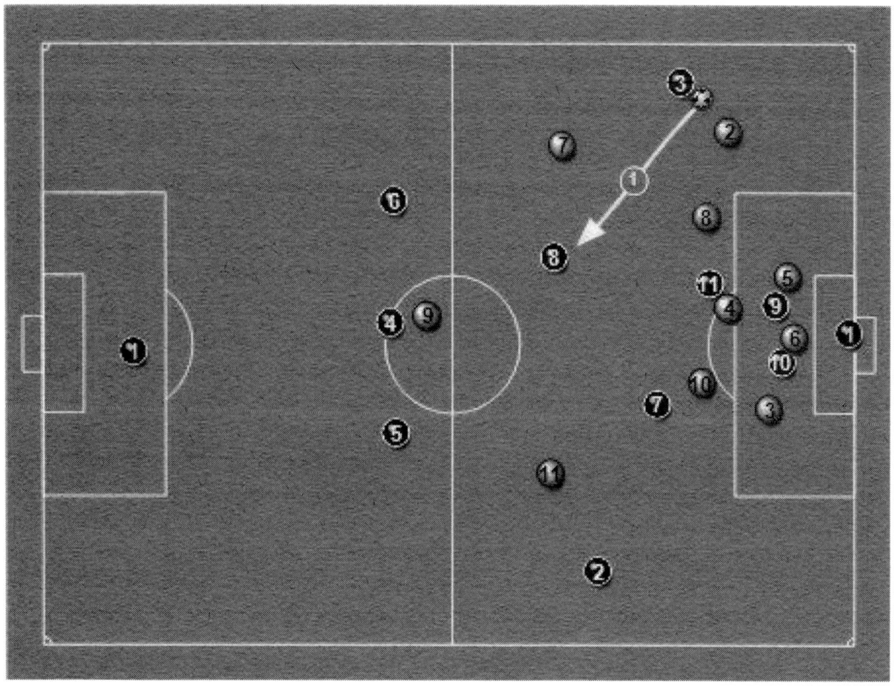

.....and it is the job of the 8 to effect this hence his positioning initially. As he presses up, in order for the team to have balance and negate the potential switched ball, the left winger, 11, must recognise the danger of the right wing back of the 352, 2, and step back into a position which deters 8 from passing the ball to him.

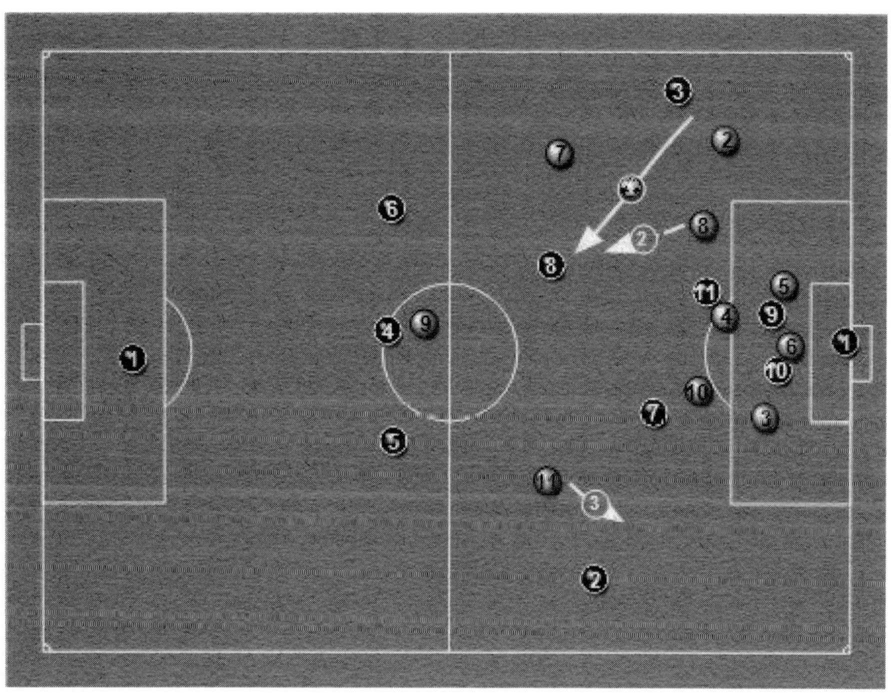

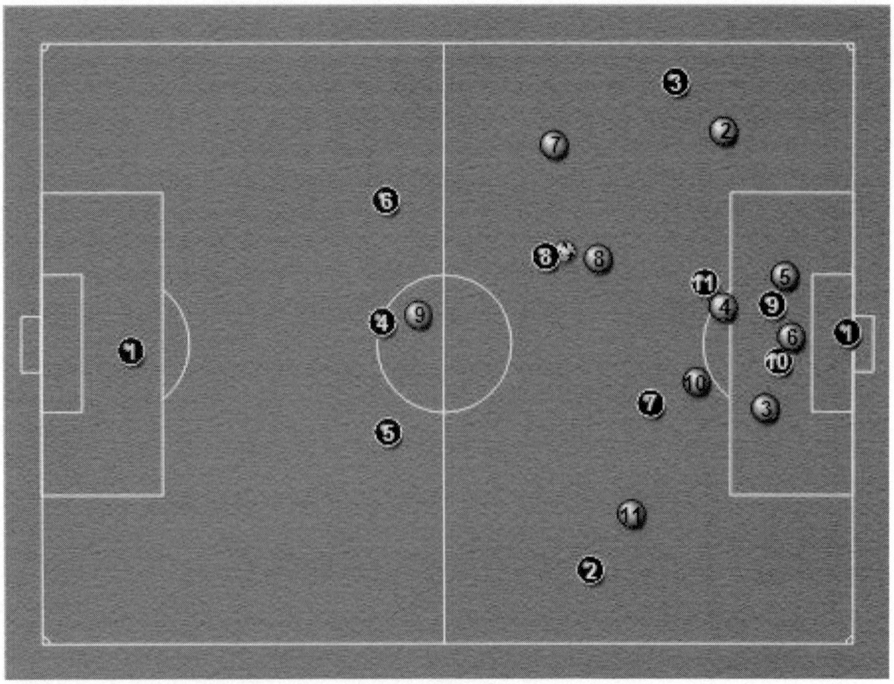

If 3 crosses the ball into the penalty area, it is vital that players are marked and not spaces which will give the bets chance of winning the first header.

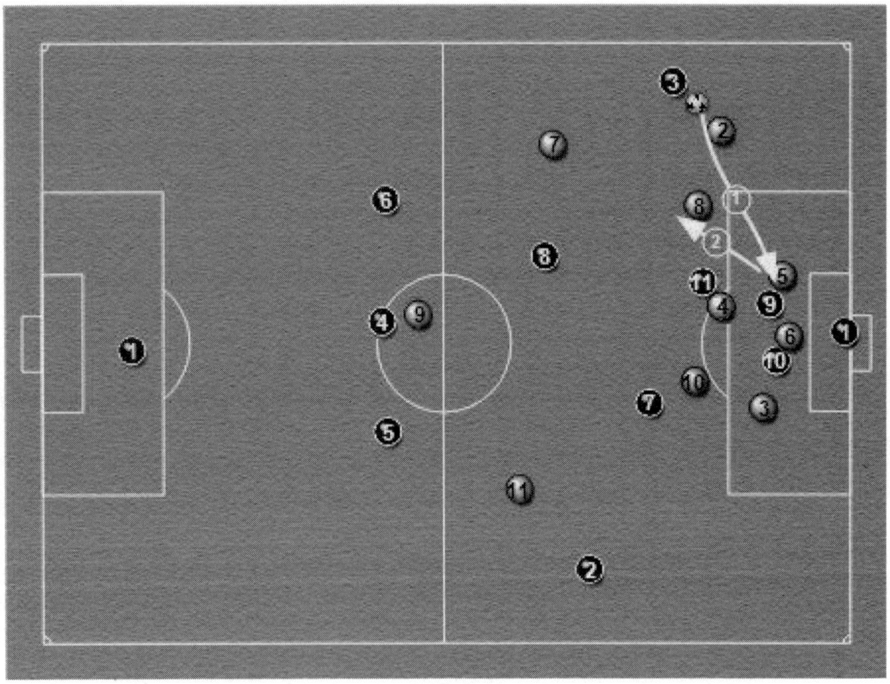

By not having the wingers, 7 & 11, dropping too deep to undertake defensive duties we have a prime opportunity from here to be able to counter attack and take advantage of the 352's unbalanced shape.

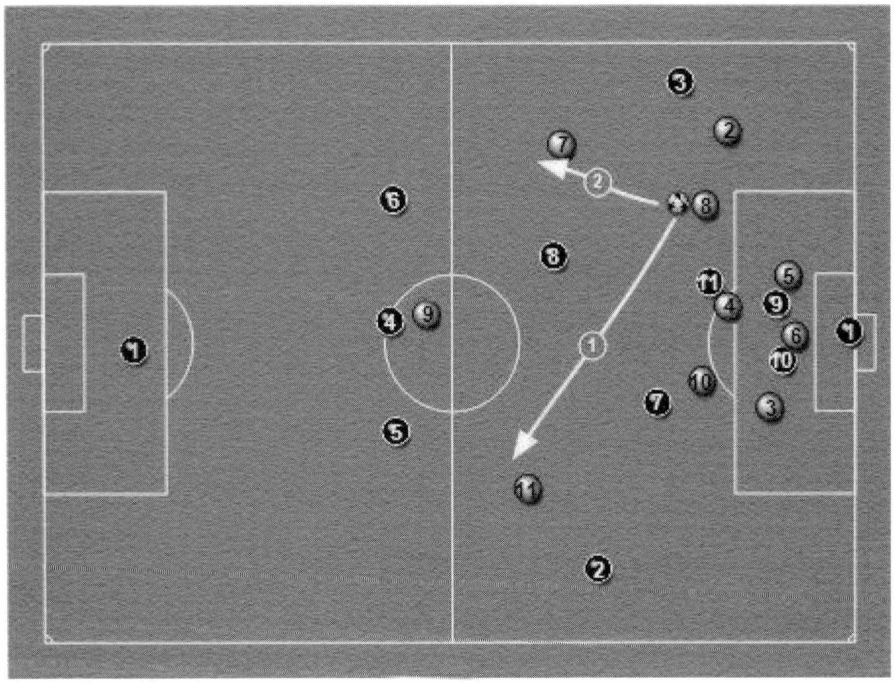

CHAPTER 8

Practices for Defending in the Defending Third

1

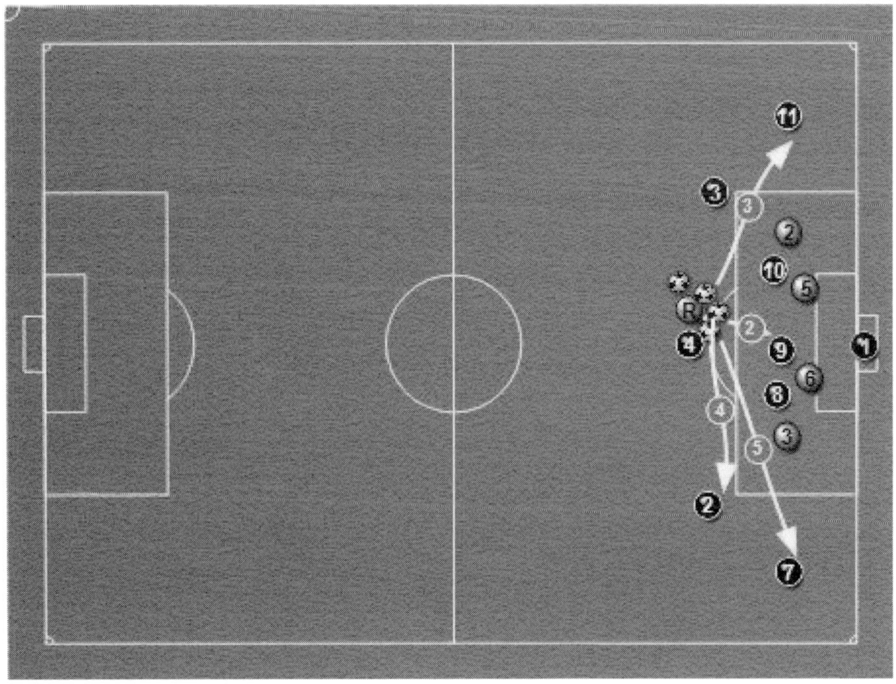

Serve the balls randomly as shown.
Defenders should stop crosses, block shots, etc.
Must defend 6 in a row or go back to zero.

CHAPTER 9

ATTACKING AGAINST THE 3-5-2

Defending Third

When we have the ball in the defensive third with the goalkeeper, obviously we have the option of kicking it long into the opponents half. However, if we are looking to play out from the back then we first have to look to set up our attacking shape. A typical 4-3-3 attacking shape would resemble the following and although the back 4 spread out in this manner enables us to initiate play from the back, the fact that the 3-5-2 has effectively got 5 midfield players against our 3 means it is difficult to get the ball from the defensive third into the mid third in a simple non risk way. In the final third of the pitch we have 3 against 3 which will lead to the wing backs of the 3-5-2 dropping slightly deeper to afford some cover, but this still leaves us man for man against the 3-5-2 central midfielders and clever rotation is needed to be able to get a player free on the ball.

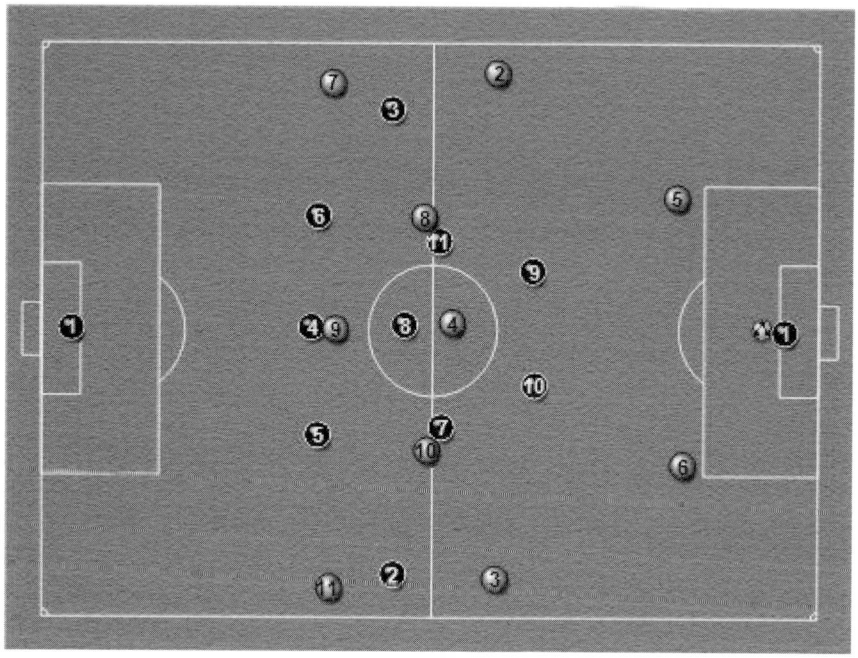

As the ball is played to 5 from the goalkeeper, although he has the option of passing to the right full back, 2, the 3-5-2 is well set up to defend against this.

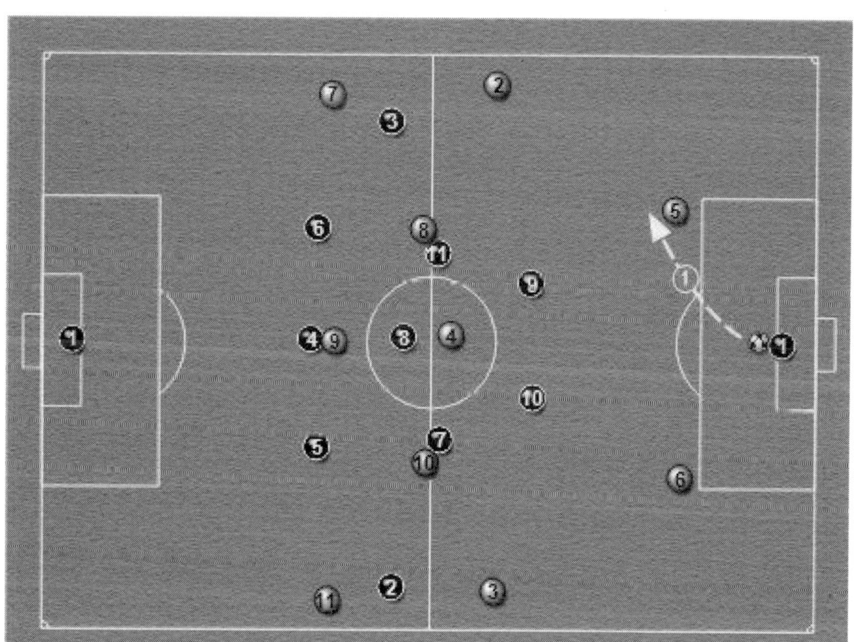

By simple, short movements from the players of the 3-5-2 they can effectively shut down the options we have of playing out from the back successfully.

Any pass that 5 now makes becomes a risky one as all of the options 5 has are covered by players of the 3-5-2.

In order to take advantage of one of the 3-5-2's weaknesses, that of the lack of support in wide areas, I have used a tactic that brazil used in the World Cup of 2002 which at first glance looks to be very elaborate but is in fact fairly routine and simple and will cause problems for the 3-5-2. The key to this is the central midfield player who initiates the movement by dropping back to the penalty area to receive the ball. As he does so the rest of the players move as shown.

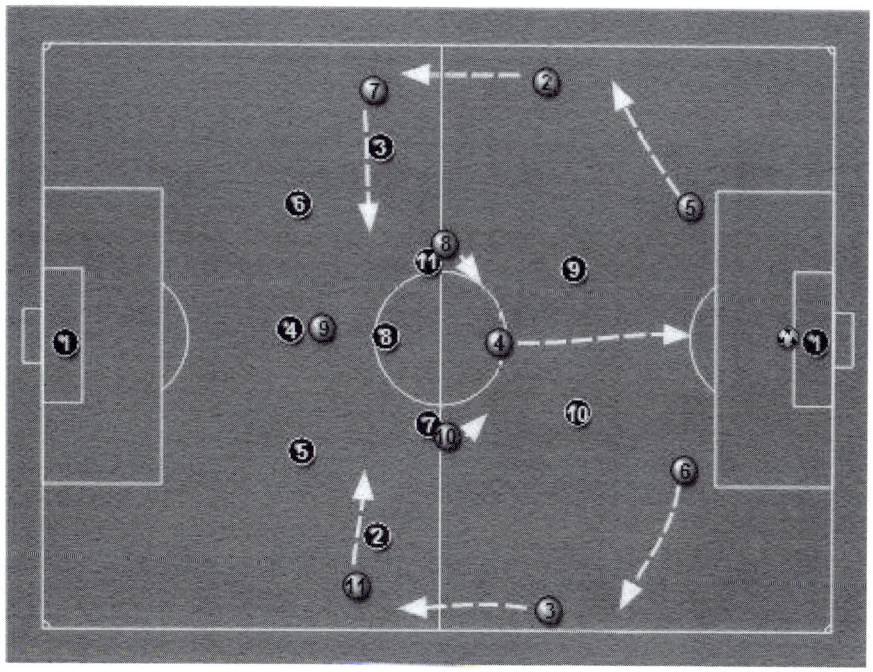

The advancement of the full backs into the threatening areas that our wingers were initially keeps the wing backs of the 3-5-2 deep. The wingers have now moved in field to create the space for the full backs to exploit at the same time as appearing in gaps in between the midfield and defense of the 3-5-2. At the back, instead of having a back 4 we now have a back 3.

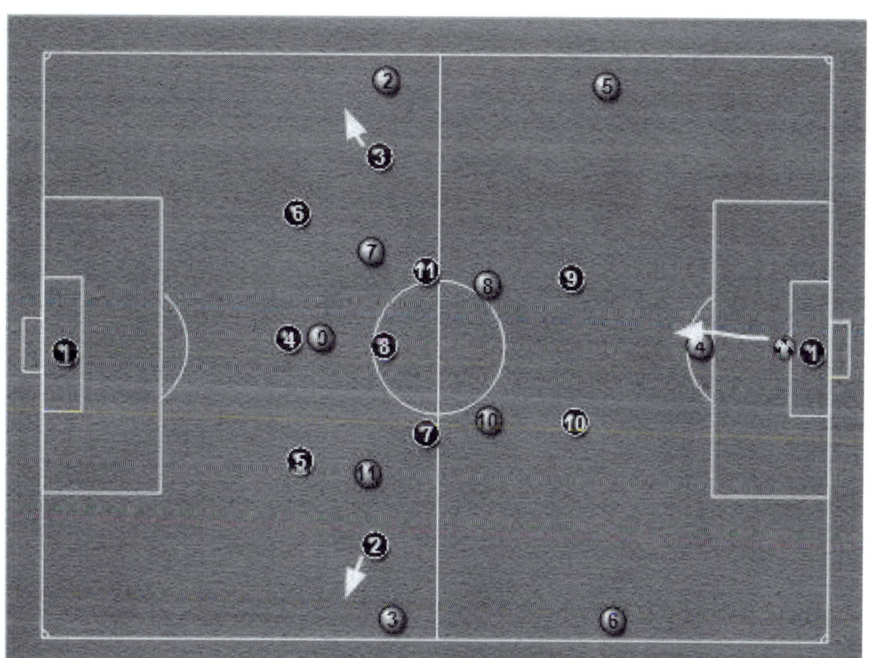

On the ball 4 now has longer options to play wide to one of the centre halves who have moved into these positions. With his position being a central one, he can act as a fulcrum to make the forward players of the 3-5-2 have to chase more if they are to be successful in closing the ball down.

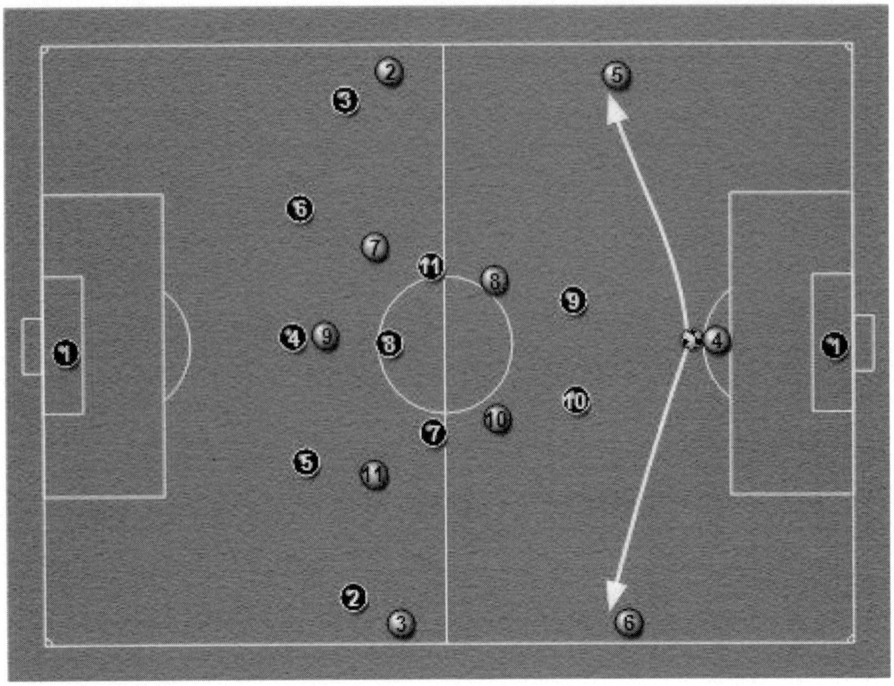

Even if the forward players do close down effectively, by using the fulcrum player to switch the ball whenever this happens, eventually one of the wide players will have time to be able to travel with the ball into the mid third.

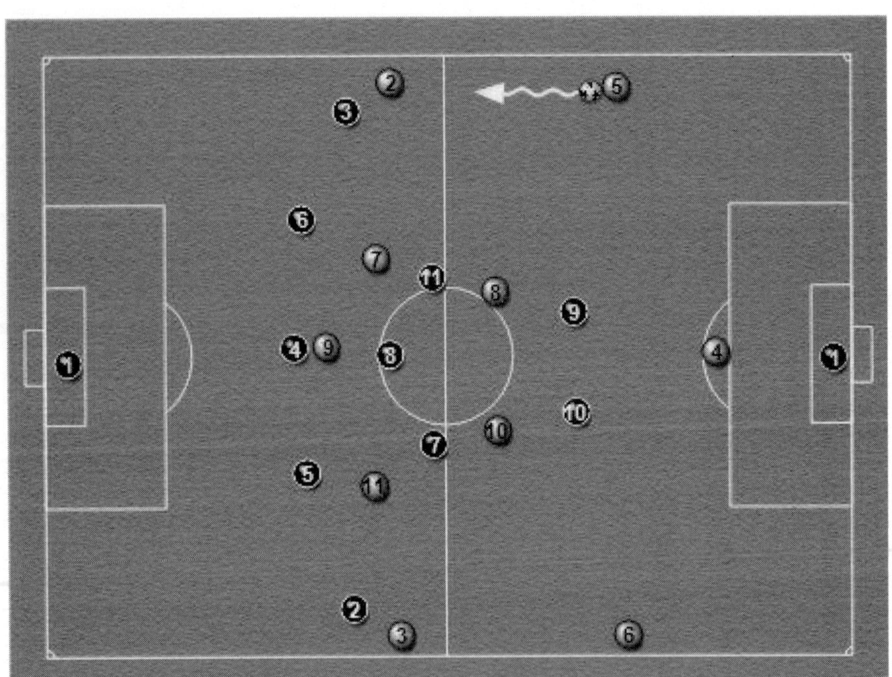

Once the scheme is effective and one of the wide central defenders travels into the mid third, in order to secure the movement defensively, the other 2 central defenders filter round to mark the forwards of the 3-5-2.

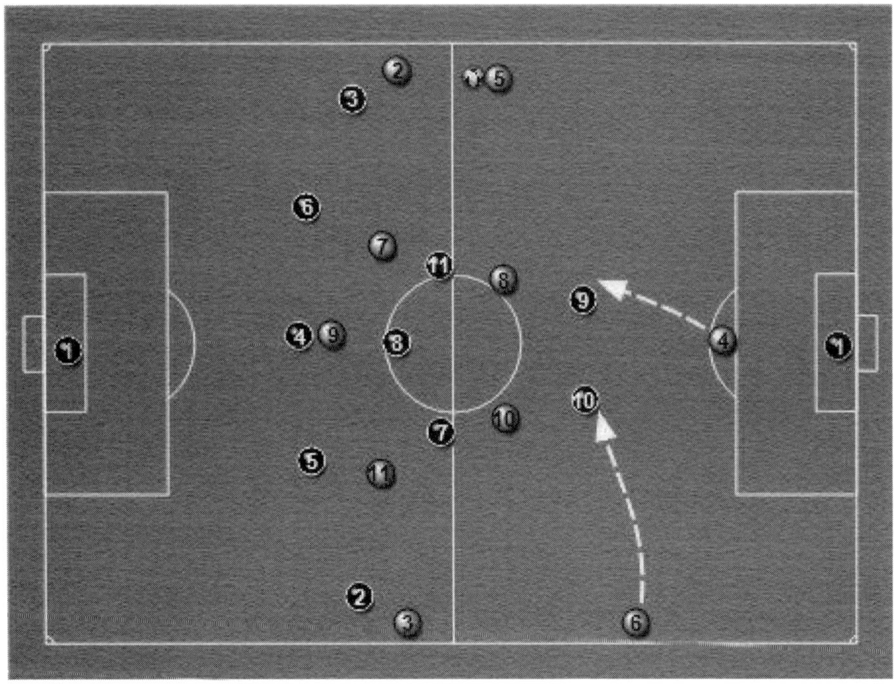

The ball is now in the mid third with a player with time and space and the offensive movement is defended.

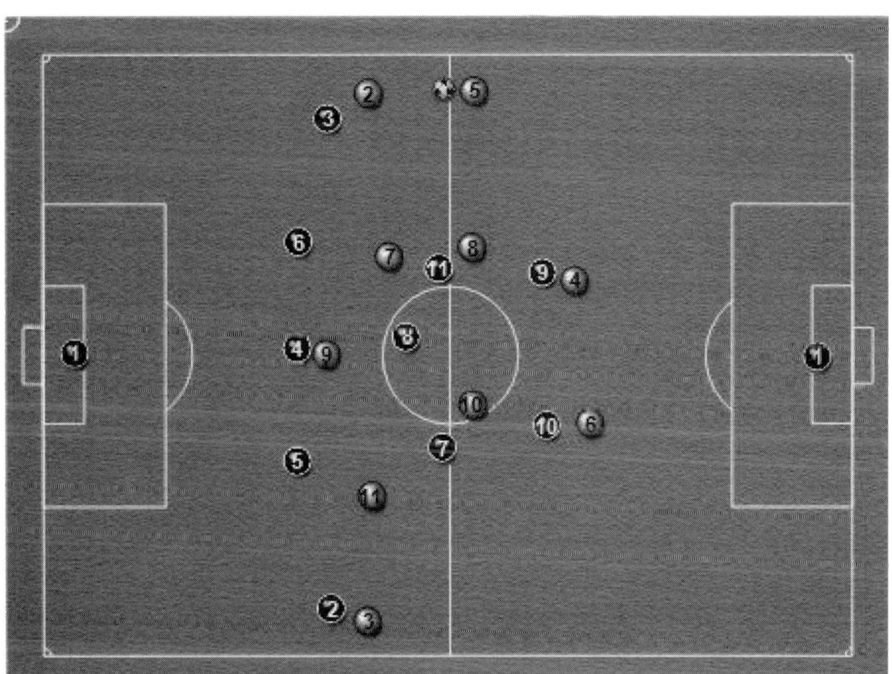

If this type of movement continues to be successful then eventually the forward players will position themselves wider to negate the travelling forward of the wide central defenders.

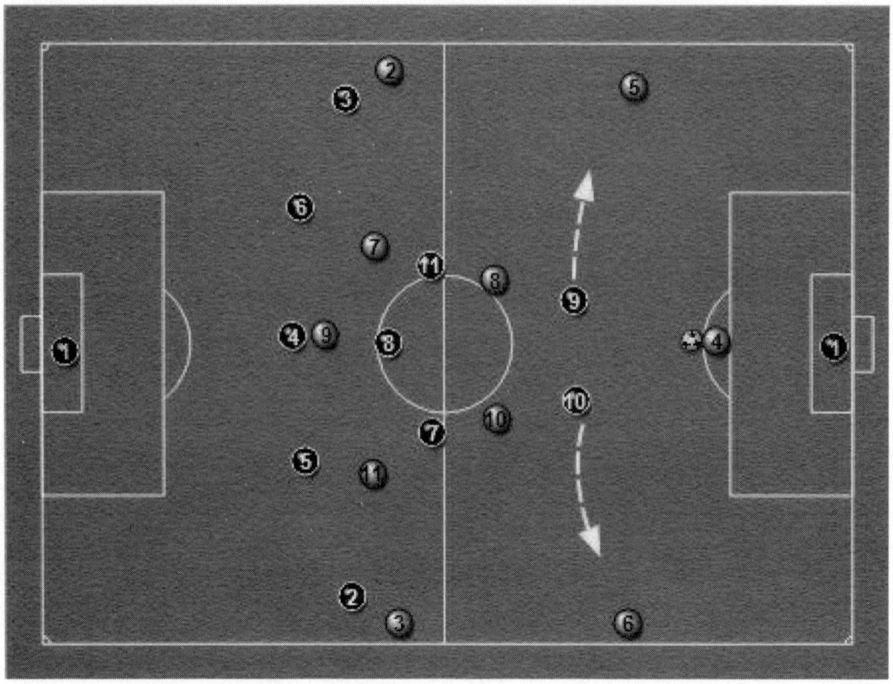

Although this negates the wider central defenders, it opens up the gate for the central defender, 4, to travel through the middle of them and appear in the mid third with time and space on the ball, aided by the spreading movement of the 2 central midfield players.

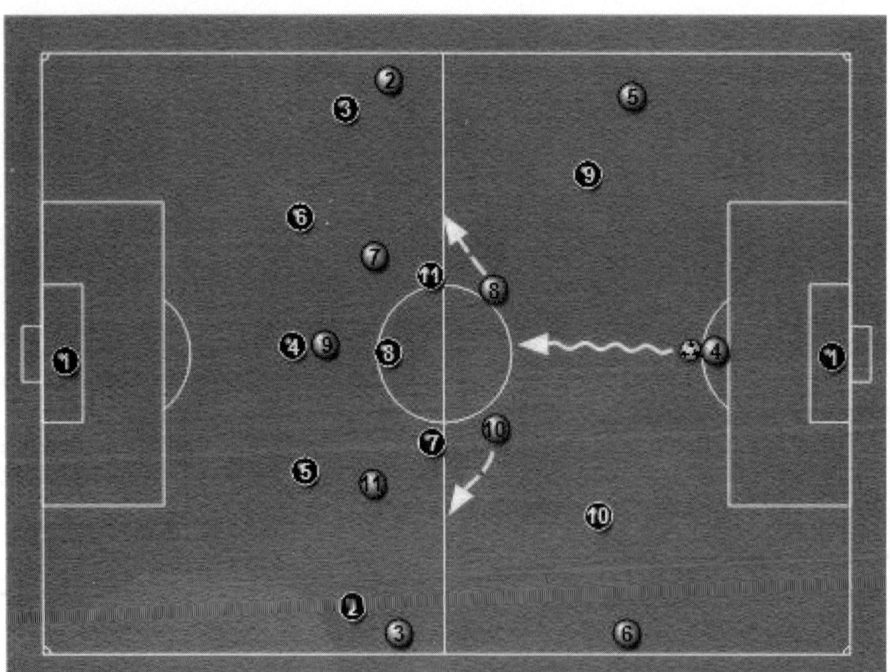

Again the movement of one of the 3 defenders into the mid third has to be covered and the remaining 2 move round to cover and mark the forward players.

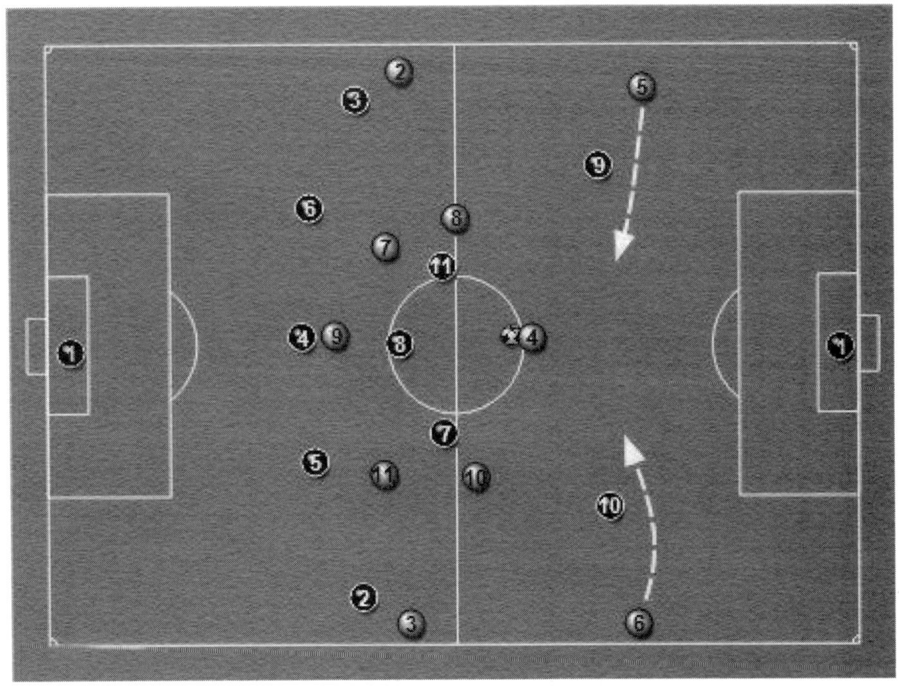

Giving us the following picture.

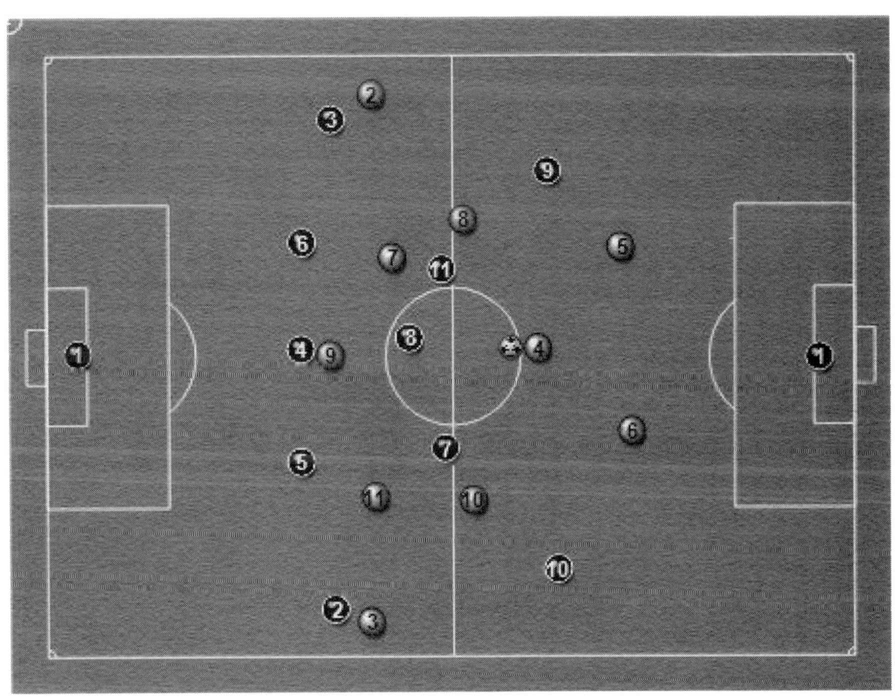

CHAPTER 10

Practices for Attacking from the Defensive Third

This is a progression of drills not only to practice how we are going to play out from the defensive third but also to convince the players of its merits.

In the first drill we have an extra man in both the defensive third and the mid third. The ball must travel through the thirds. Due to the extra player we have the players will find it easy to transfer the ball into the attacking third where, as would happen in a game, the space becomes less and players are tighter to their men making it more difficult to score a goal.

Once the players are finding it easy to get the ball into the attacking third, progress to the next level where the 4-3-3 shape is more evident. The players will find it more difficult to play out from the back with this shape due to the lack of an extra man in the mid third. Progress this drill on so that a player may travel with the ball into the next third and may not be followed.

Finally, show the movement we have created to play out from the back in the last drill and again this should be easier to get into the attacking third without the aid of the extra man.

1

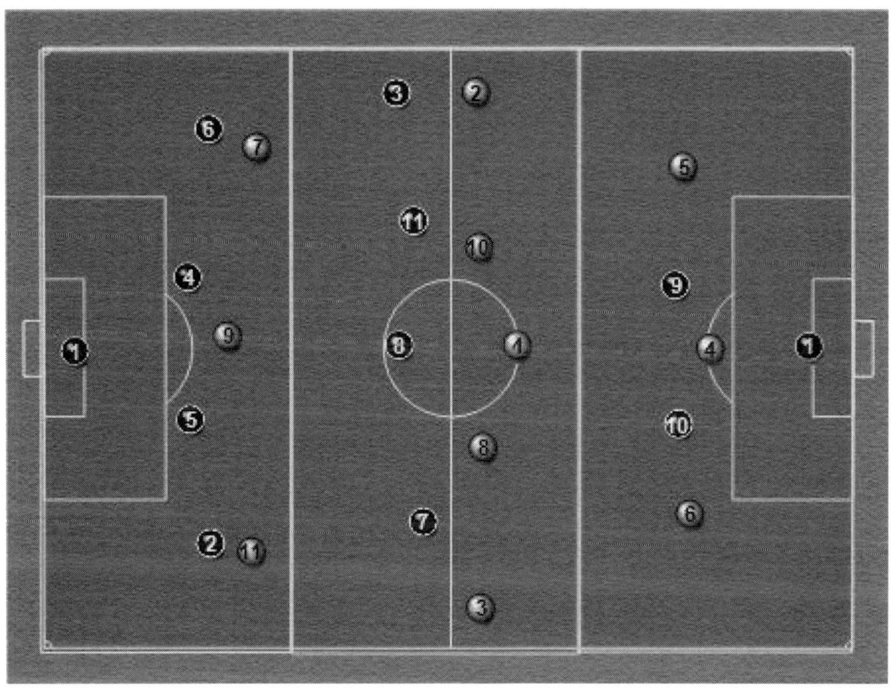

2

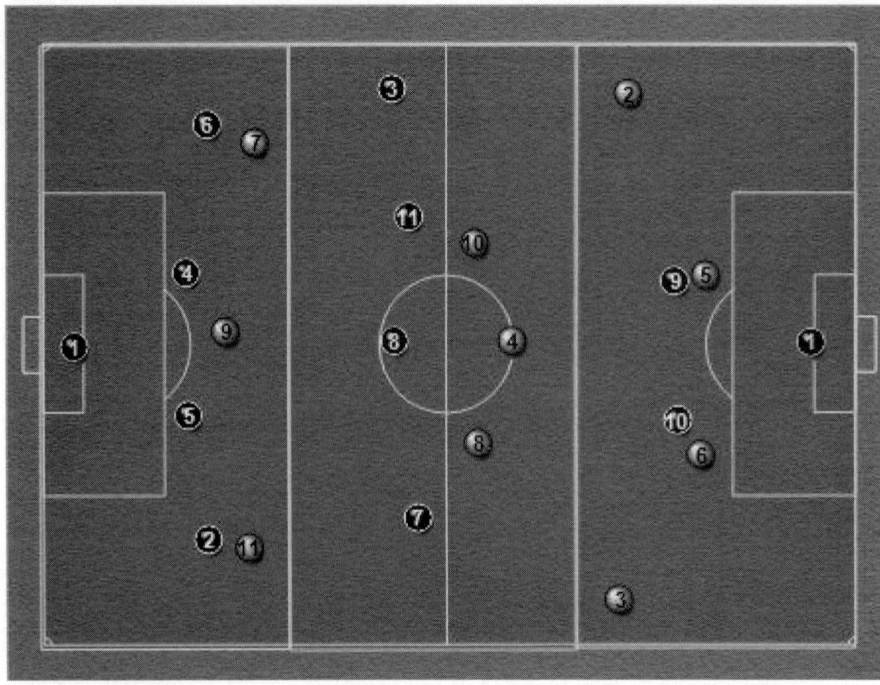

3

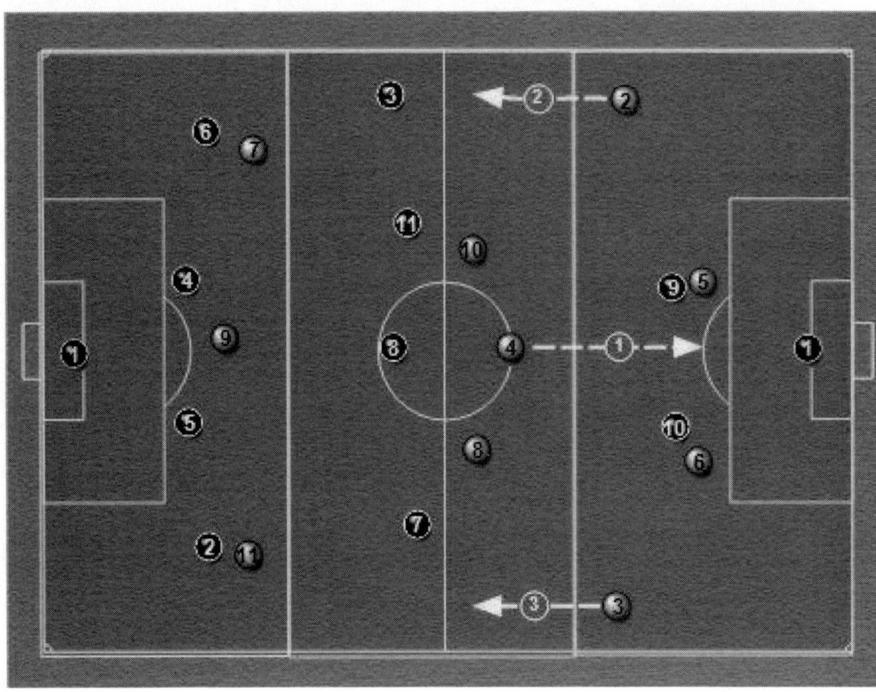

4

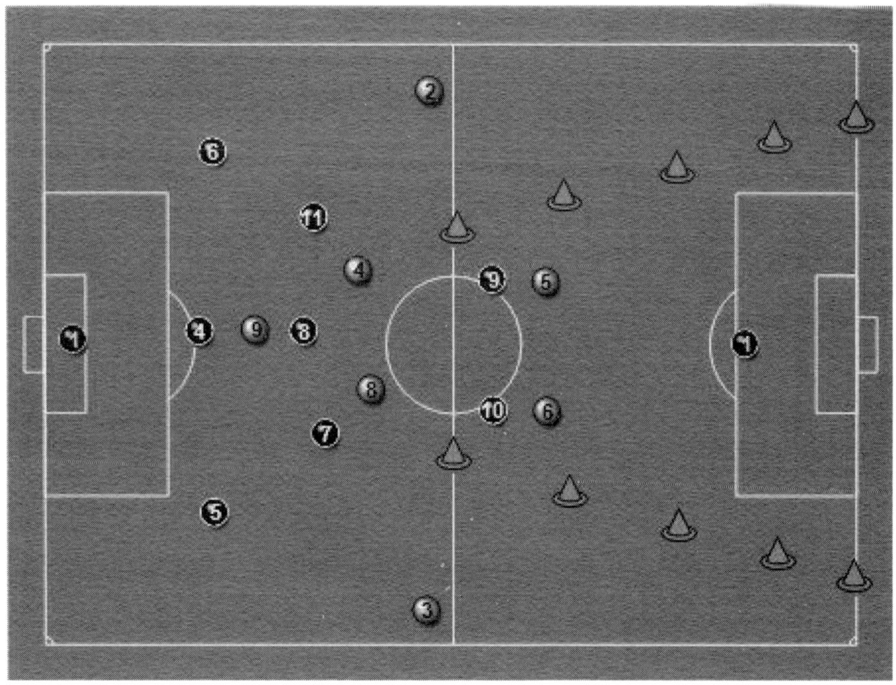

Practice for 2 v 2 defending.
No other players are allowed in coned area other than 2 forwards and 2 defenders + Goalkeeper.
Start with opposition goalkeeper.

CHAPTER 11

ATTACKING AGAINST THE 3-5-2

Mid Third

By demonstrating a very effective way of getting into the mid third from the defensive third we now have to address how to pass or run the ball successfully into the final third. Establishing the principle of one of the 3 defenders who initiated the attack progressing with the ball into the mid third, the 3-5-2 system has to deal with this and would probably do so in the manner shown, with the 3 central midfielders shuffling over to meet the man on the ball and balance off the team. At this point it is worth noting the 2v2 situation we have defensively at the back, with the 2 strikers of the 352 system marked by defenders 4 & 6 in this instance. This is a bold tactic though with the screen in front of these 2 players made up of 8 & 10, it enables the defenders to not have to get so tight to forward players and as such they are favourites to win the race for any counter attack pass made into the space behind them. Offensively the further advancement of our 2 pushes the left wing of the 3-5-2, number 3, deeper.

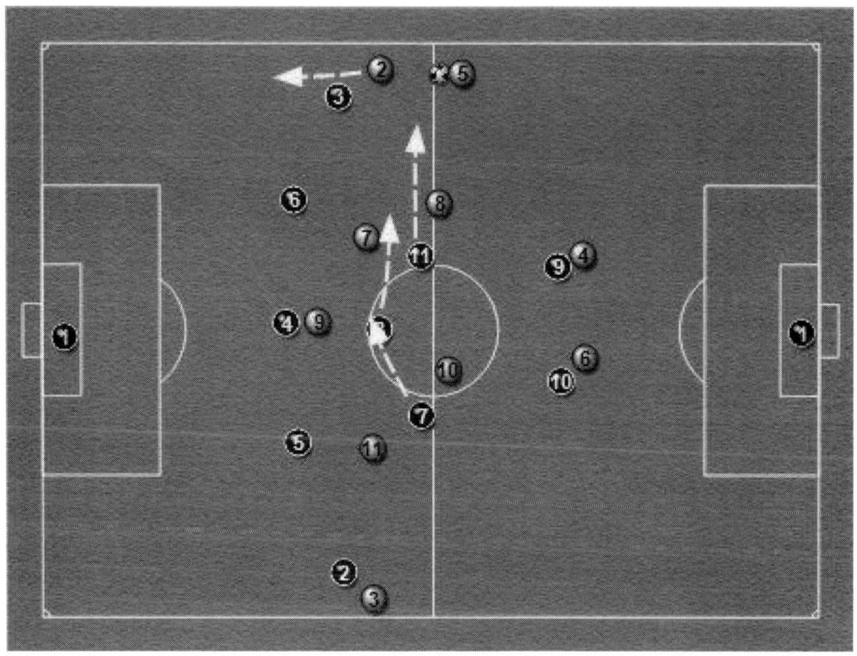

As the central midfield players of the 3-5-2 shuffle over it is important that our forward players move as shown to continue to give options to the man on the ball and problems for the defending players of the 3-5-2.

If the player closing the ball down shows outside, ie; the touchline, we have the following scenario that can unveil…

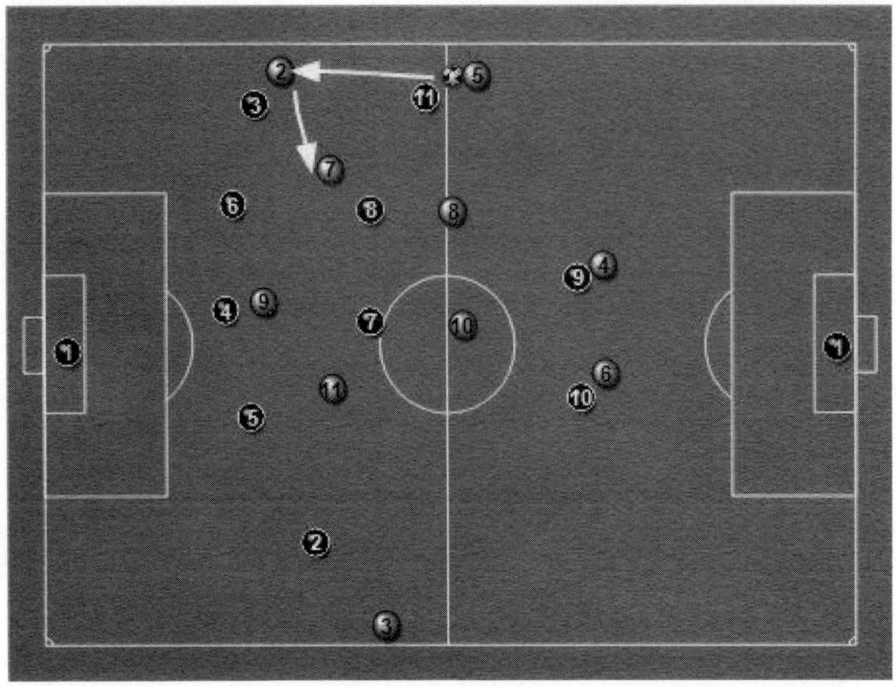

...which creates space in which 7 can then attack the final third either by running with the ball or passing.

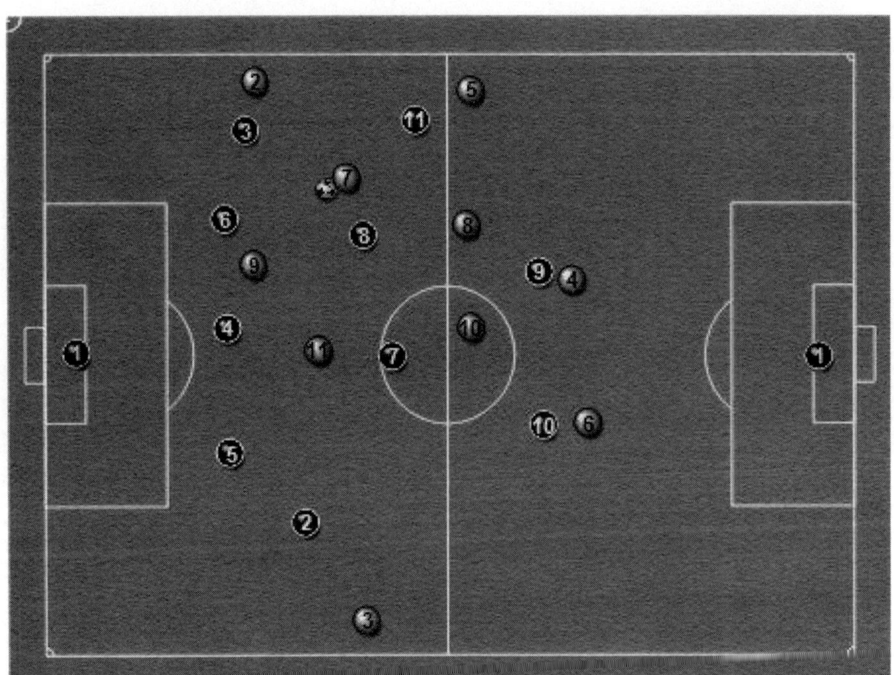

Or if the player closing the ball down shuts off the potential pass down the touchline then an option is opened up for 5 to pass inside to the anchor player of our midfield, who may then have forward options as shown here...

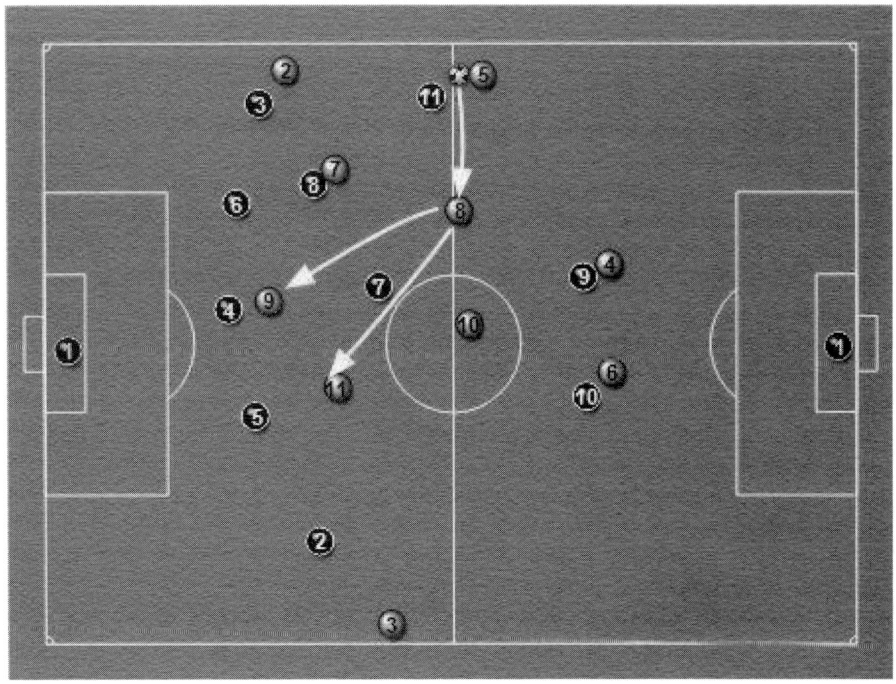

...or if those forward options are closed off then he will be able to switch the ball effectively to the other side.

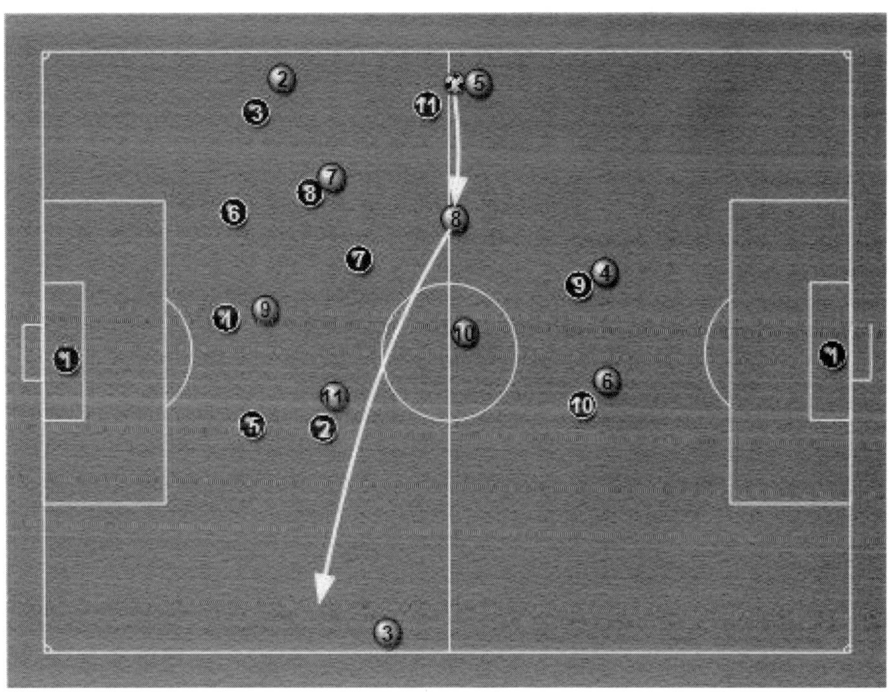

Dependent on how the opposition close the options down, there may even be the possibility of searching in behind the defense of the 3-5-2 with a longer pass for the striker.

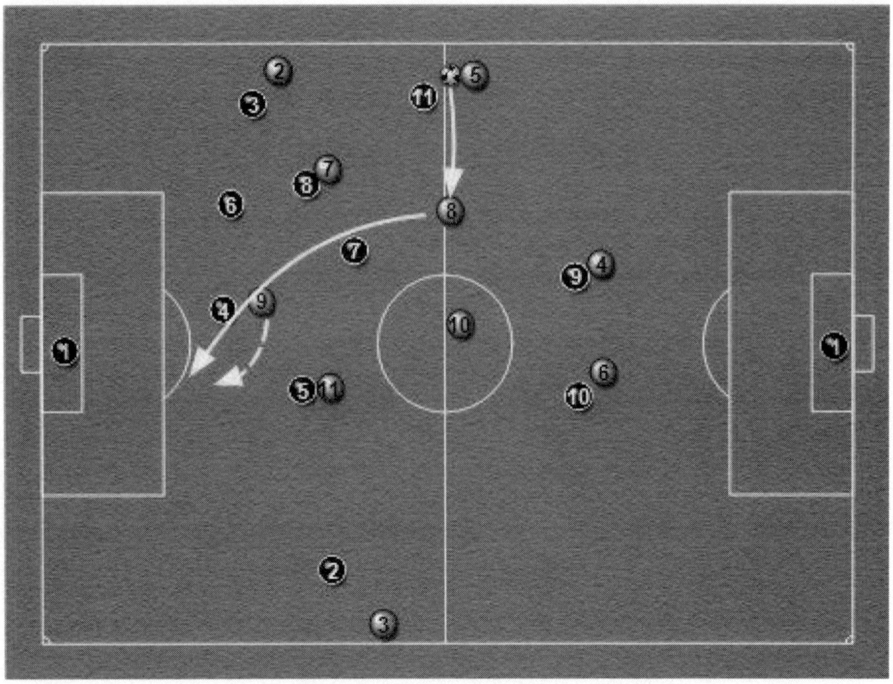

As we showed in the defending third chapter, it may be that the progression of one of the wide central defenders is halted which would open up the possibility of the central defender to progress into the mid third. If this happens and he is allowed to progress unopposed to the position shown then the passing options for him are numerous as shown.

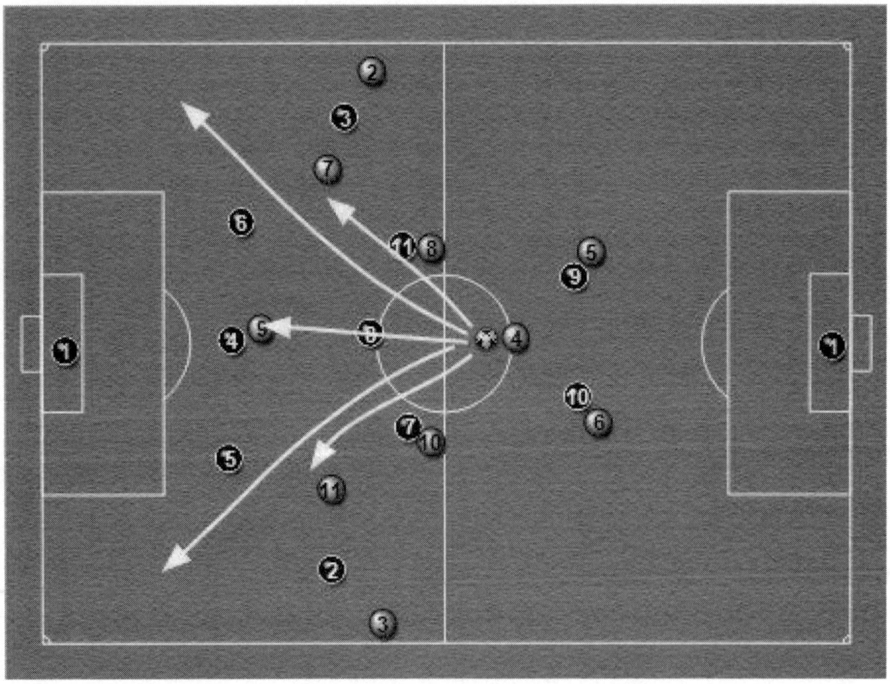

Having come inside form the touchline, the original wingers in our system can receive the ball from the advancing central defender who is being closed down and get into a similar position as shown previously from where they can begin to penetrate the final third.

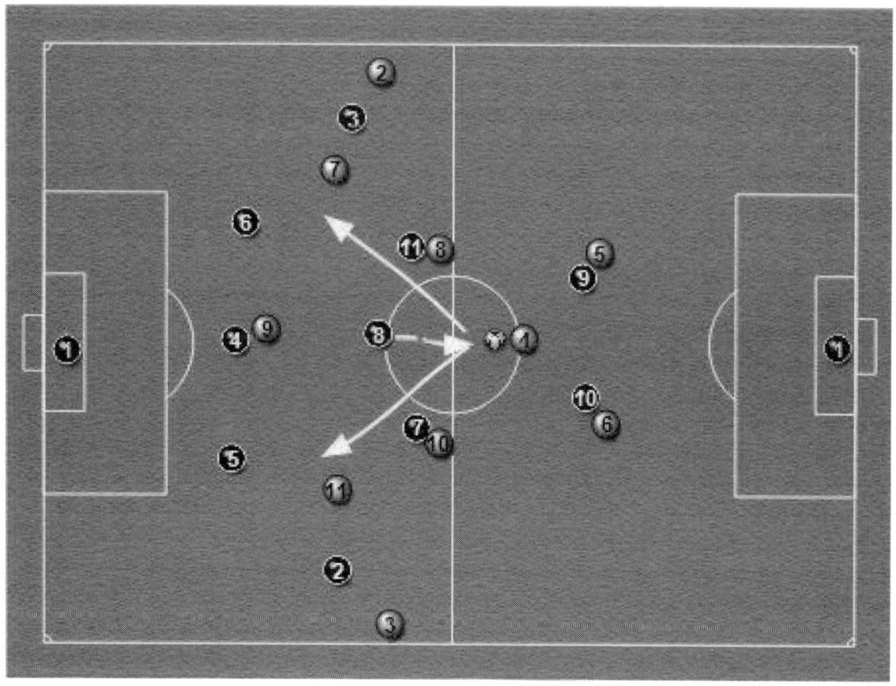

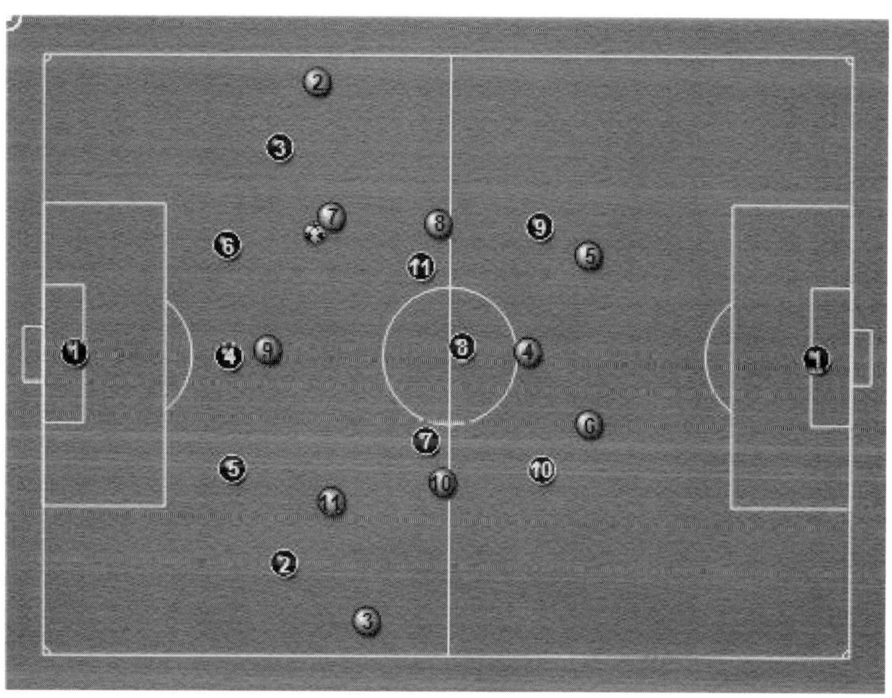

If the player who closes down comes from a different angle as he is doing here then the passing option is still opened up.

Which creates the same scenario but on the opposite side.

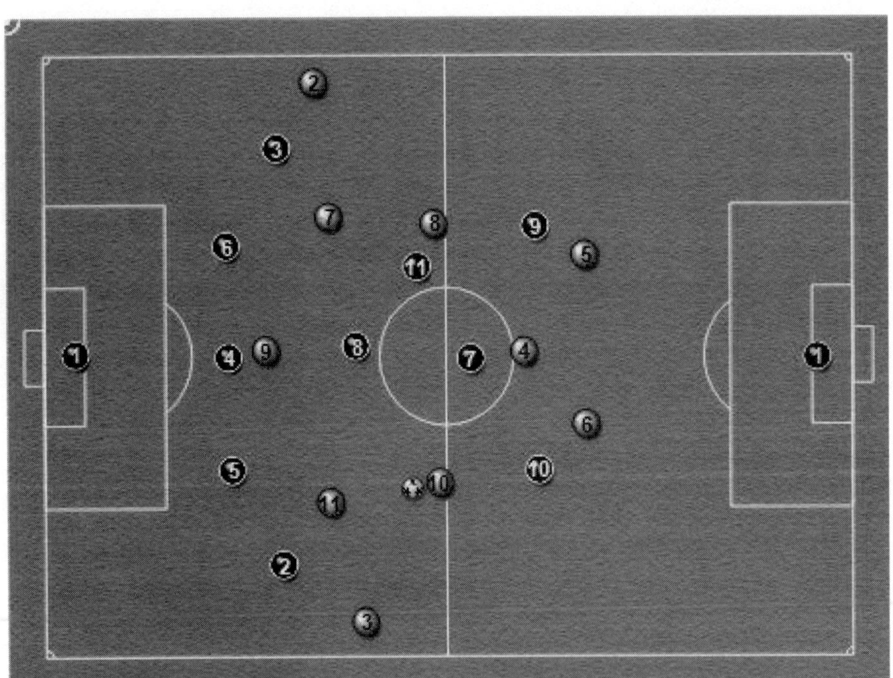

Should one of the defenders of the 3-5-2 system choose to negate this passing option by coming out of his zone to mark the winger who has come inside then the longer ball into the space created for the striker is opened up.

Giving him an opportunity to get a strike in on goal.

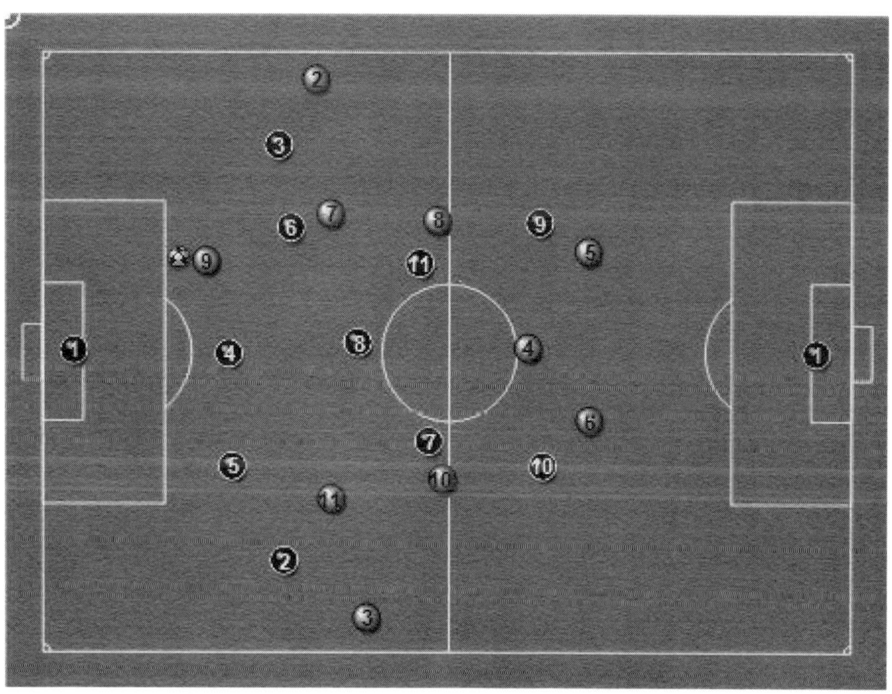

Should the 3-5-2 system drop even deeper because of the forward passing options for the man on the ball then he should not be afraid to progress even further with the ball, but the other central midfield players should ensure that cover is given to him behind as he does this.,

This then gives us sufficient cover in front of the 2 defending players enabling them to be happier being 2 against 2 with the forward players of the 3-5-2.

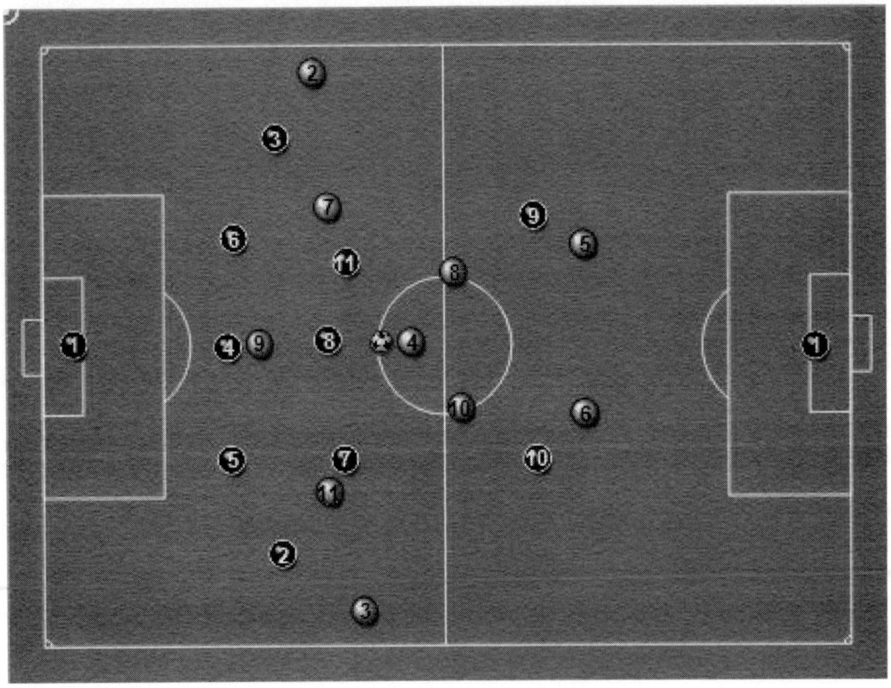

CHAPTER 12

Practices for Attacking from the Mid Third

1

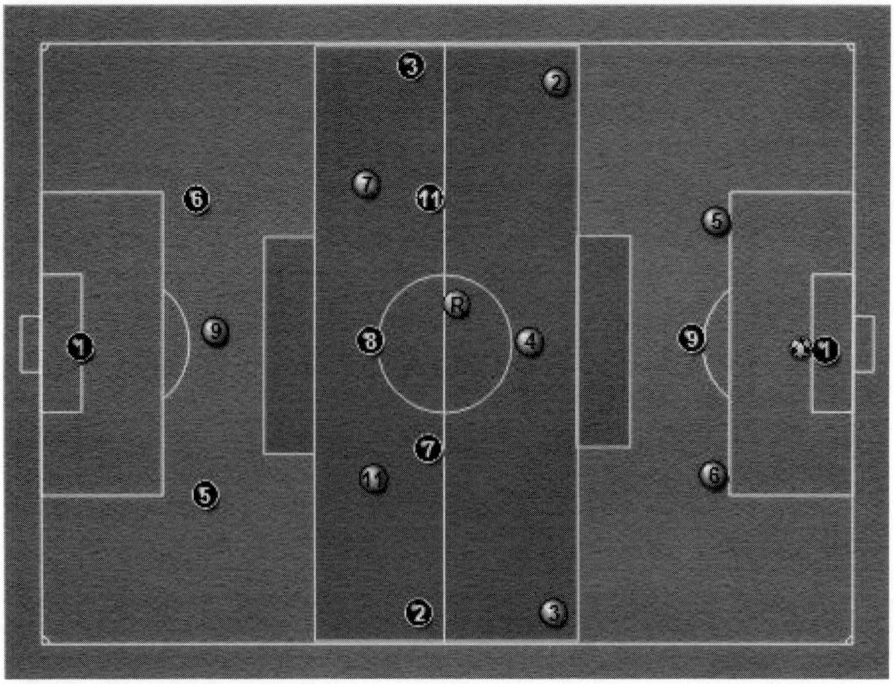

Must play through the thirds.
Player from the mid third must receive in the end shaded area in order to then go and attack 2 v2.

2

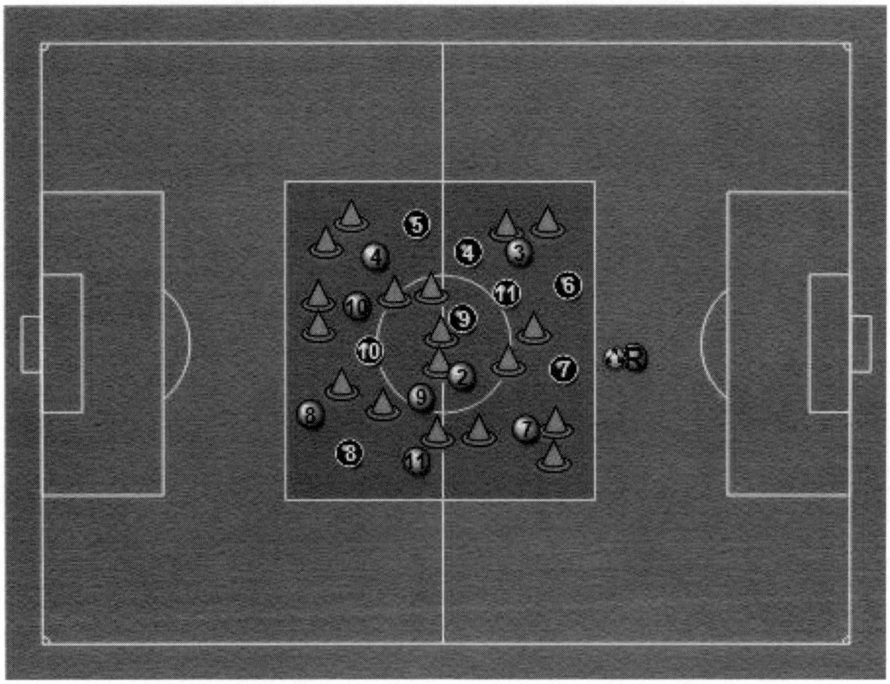

Play 8 v 8 in the area with 9 goals 1 yard apart.
There will always be a goal free which encourages the switched play.

3

Play with 2 goals facing the ‘wrong’ way.
Either team can score in either goal.
Objective is to switch the play to the lesser defended goal.

CHAPTER 13

ATTACKING AGAINST THE 3-5-2

Attacking Third

Once we get into the final third our objective has to be to hurt the 3-5-2 as quickly as possible before it has time to regroup and become resolute and get too many players behind the ball. The attitude of 7 in this instance has to be to commit the defenders of the 3-5-2 into making a decision by running directly at them.

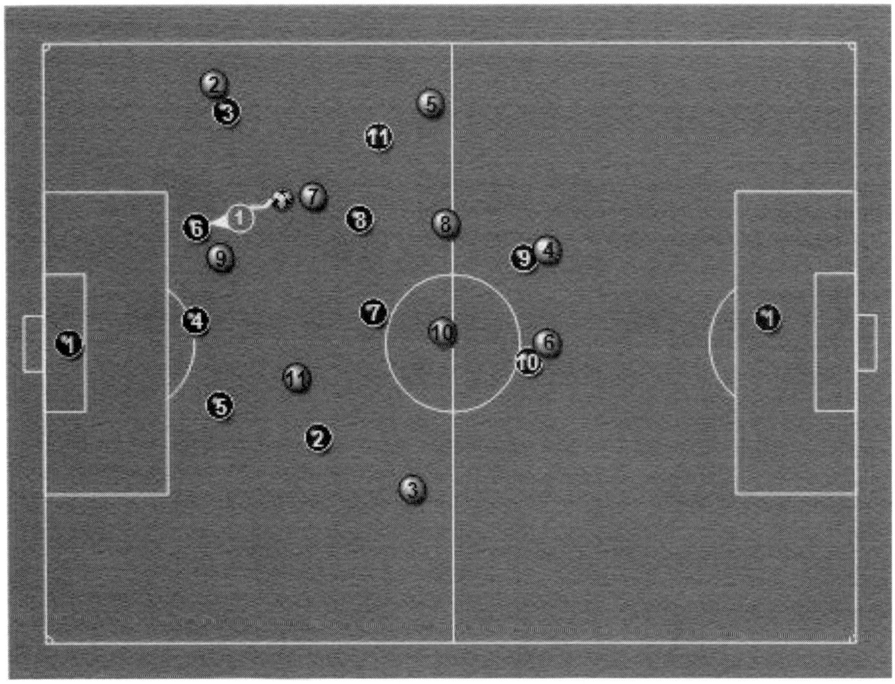

As one defender comes out to close him down this creates space which can be exploited behind the defense of the 3-5-2, with either the advancing right full back, 2, getting in behind ready to cross the ball or a pass that is slid down the side of the oncoming defender for 9 to get a strike on goal.

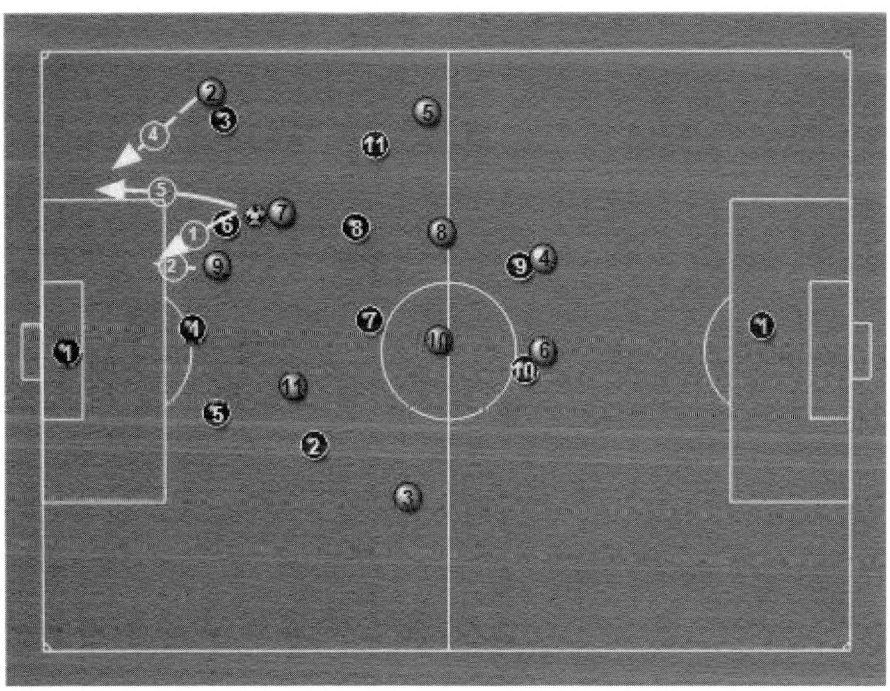

Should the whole back 3 defenders of the 3-5-2 manage to close off the spaces that can be exploited, this should open up the gap for our 11 to get into around the back of them.

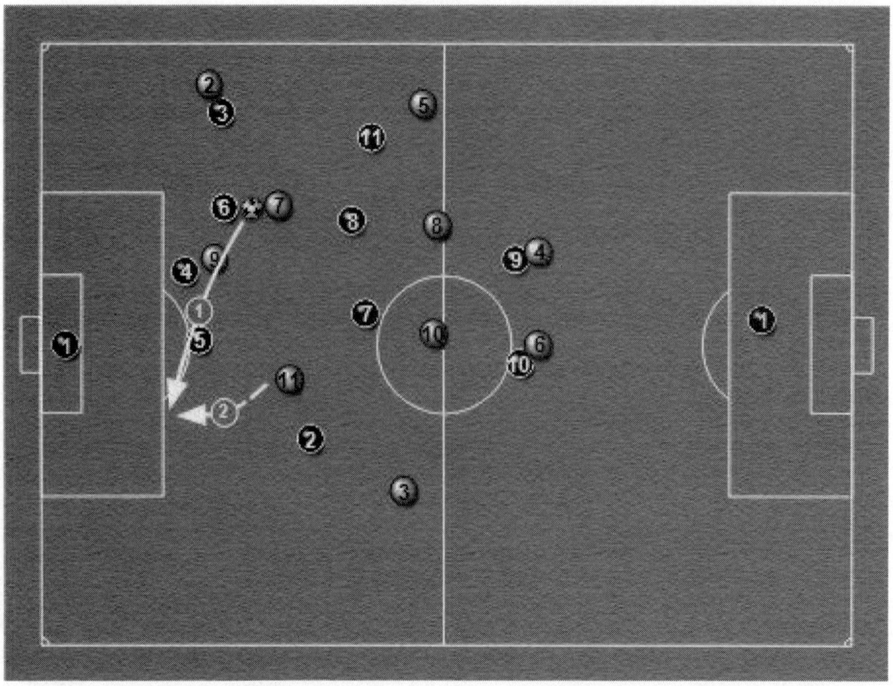

If they are good enough to close this option off too then the opposite full back, 3, can get into the hole created for the ball to be switched.

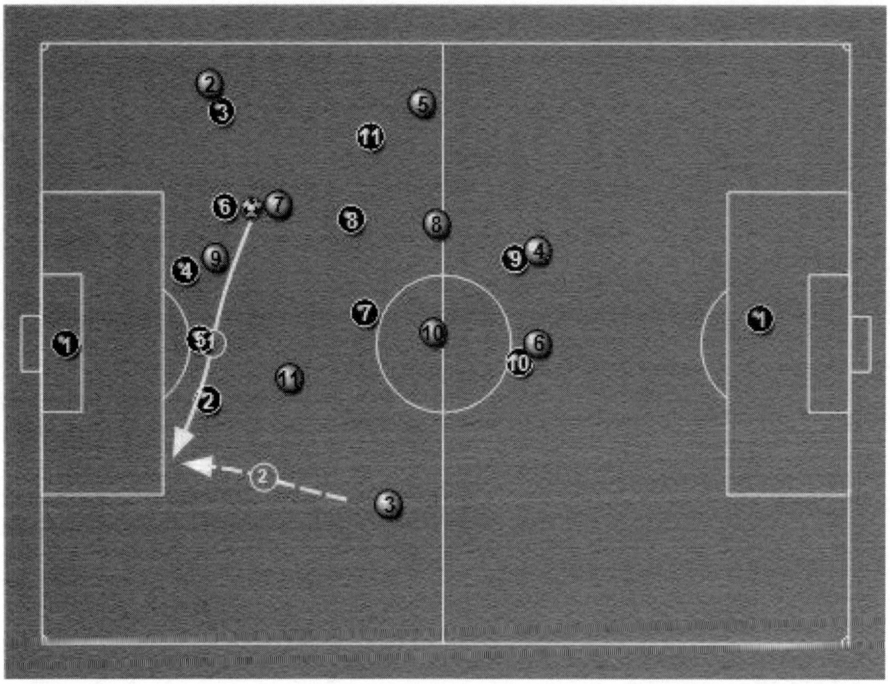

If cleverer movement is required then the following option is available by utilising a simple cross over run to give 7 more options on the ball.

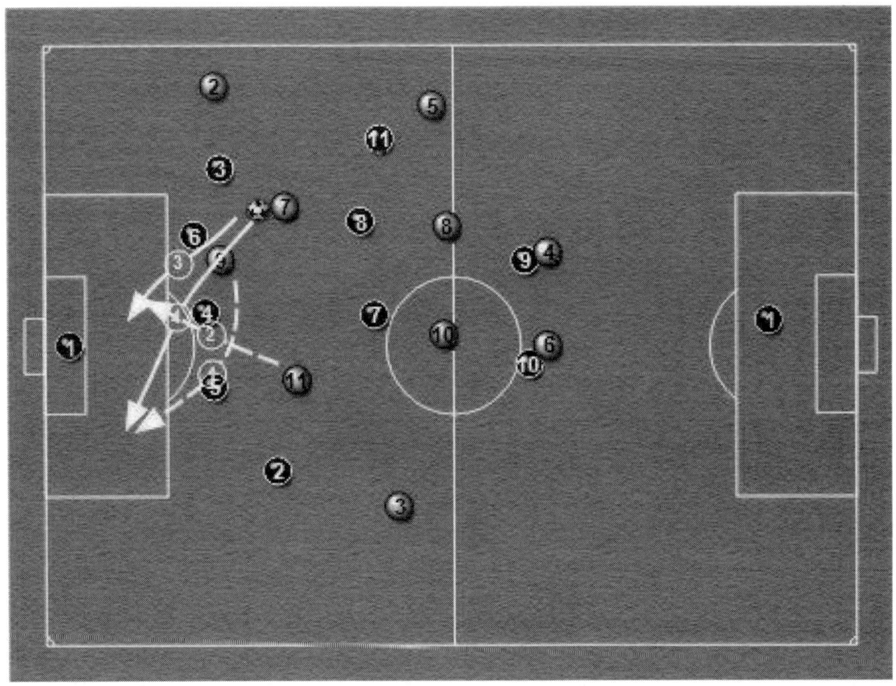

CHAPTER 14

Practices for attacking in the final third

1

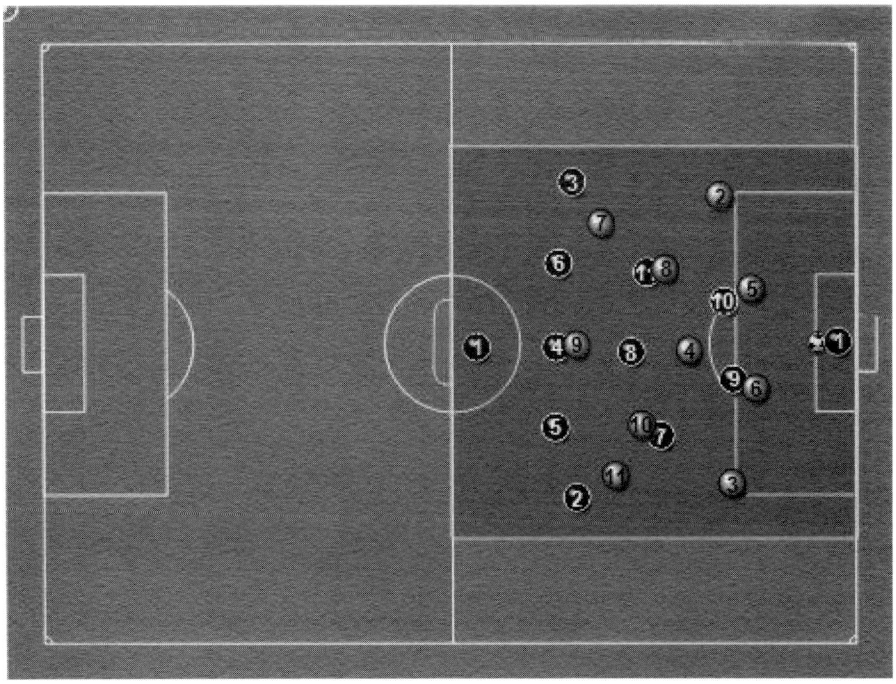

Play 10 v 10 in the small area shown to promote quick bright play needed in the final third.

2

Coach feeds the ball alternately to either player as shown.
Striker makes a spin run to make space for a strike at goal.

3

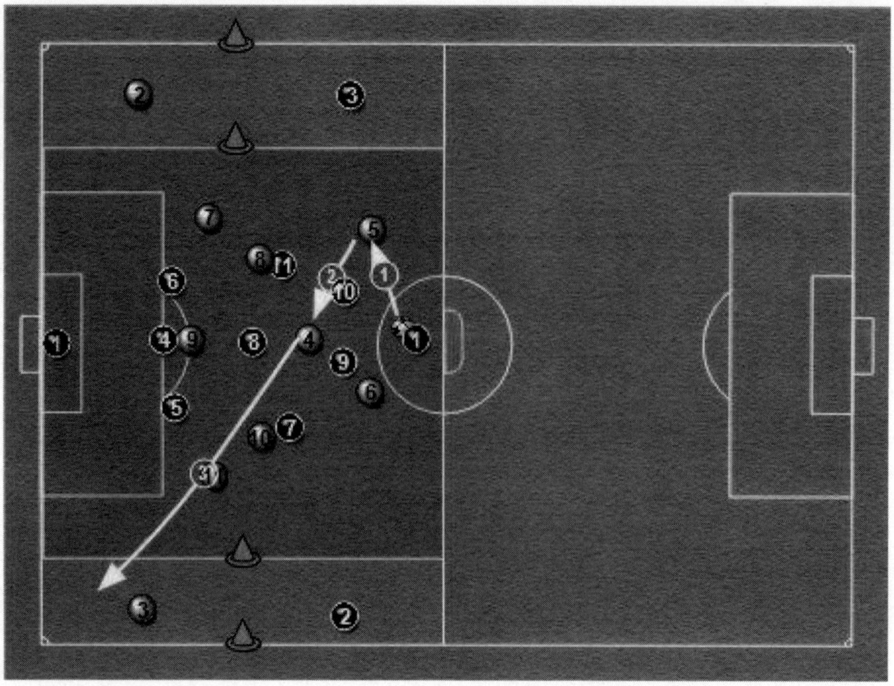

Ball must be passed a minimum of twice prior to transferring into wide areas for cross.

CONCLUSION

I believe that to play effectively against the 3-5-2 system there is a need to be bold and ask questions of the back 3 players. For this reason I have chosen to play with a formation against the 3-5-2 which utilises 3 forward players, forcing the wing backs to retreat and provide more cover when we are in possession of the ball. Notwithstanding this, without any movement from the wingers of our system when we have the ball the lone striker would become extremely isolated. It becomes fundamental to our offensive schemes therefore for the wide players to come infield at the correct moment, but this can only be achieved if there is a player from our formation who is replacing the wingers position out wide in order to continue to give problems for the wing back of the 3-5-2. The offensive playing out from the back that Brazil utilised in the World Cup of 2002 is an excellent aid to give the full backs of our system the licence to get into very advanced areas to do this. Although it may seem elaborate to try and coach a team to use this Brazilian tactic, it really is simple but does require players who are not only tactically efficient but also technically able to keep the ball. However, in reality this is the same for any formation. The manner with which I have set out to play against and beat the 3-5-2 system is creative but I truly believe that you will have endless amounts of fun coaching the method of it and if it is successful it will become immensely satisfying.

OTHER BOOKS IN THIS SERIES

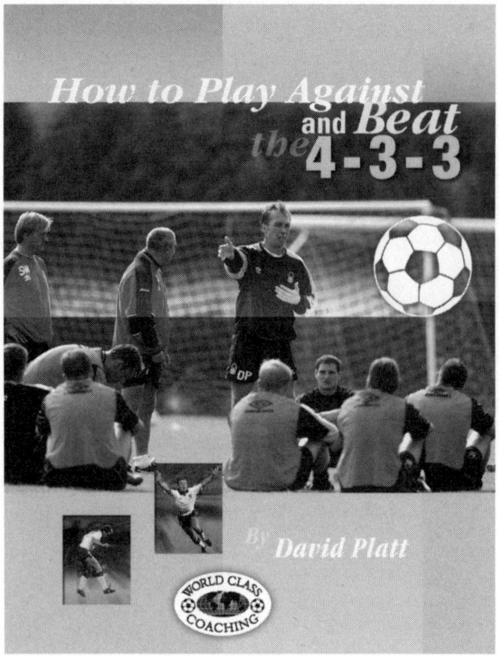

WORLD CLASS COACHING DVD's

worldclasscoaching.com or 1-888-342-6224